Successful Business Plan

DEVELOPMENT

A Process Approach

Designed for use at University of Saskatchewan

one-time online access code included

Lee A. Swanson

Kendall Hunt
publishing company

Cover image © Shutterstock.com

www.kendallhunt.com
Send all inquiries to:
4050 Westmark Drive
Dubuque, IA 52004-1840

Published in the United States of America

Table of Contents

Detailed Table of Contents

List of Figures

List of Tables

List of Tables

Acknowledgments

I am thankful for the feedback provided by undergraduate and MBA students as they used previous versions of this book. Thanks also to the many entrepreneurs, business plan and pitch competition contestants, and entrepreneurship support organisations for using this resource and providing valuable feedback. This book was designed with and for you. Thank you for your suggestions and advice.

Thanks also to the professors who reviewed the book and provided valuable suggestions for its improvement, including Tyler Case, Brooke Klassen, and Grant Wilson. I'm forever grateful for your help and expert insights.

As always, I appreciate the support from family and friends. Thanks to Merle and Eugene, Sherri and Cliff, Dylan and Taylor and Claire, Glenda and Darrell, Nyk and Erin, and too many others to name.

Introduction

I designed this textbook and its accompanying worksheets and business plan templates with and for students wanting a practical and easy-to-follow guide for developing a business plan. It follows a unique format that both explains what to do and demonstrates how to do it.

The book begins with a general overview of business development before describing the business planning process, how to conduct business planning research, and the essential elements of a business plan's front matter and operations, human resources, marketing, and financial plans. It explains how to determine financing needs, make the plan realistic, and how to develop it further, so it is appealing to investors and other stakeholders and desirable for the entrepreneur. The book finishes by describing how to do a business plan pitch.

One of the book's key features is the detailed and easy-to-apply process for developing business plans. The book also features a Research Analyses Worksheets tool and extensive Word and Excel templates to use to develop a business plan. Finally, a cross-chapter case spans the first 11 chapters to walk users through a realistic business plan development scenario using the worksheets and templates. The cross-chapter case also serves as a users' manual for the Business Plan Excel Template and a guide for applying the business planning process.

I hope that students, professors, entrepreneurs, and others who want to develop business plans find this book and its accompanying worksheets and templates to be of use.

Chapter 1

Developing a Business

Learning Objectives

After completing this chapter, you will be able to:

◆ Describe the stages of business development

◆ Describe the types of business development

◆ Explain the two general approaches to starting a business

◆ Describe the purposes for business planning

◆ Explain how to effectively communicate in a business plan while establishing and maintaining credibility

◆ Describe the general guidelines for developing business plans

◆ Describe the business plan development process

◆ Use the business plan templates

Overview

According to the Government of Canada (2019):

It is important to have a business plan because it helps you set realistic goals, secure external funding, measure your success, clarify operational requirements and establish reasonable financial forecasts. Preparing your plan will also help you focus on how to operate your new business and give it the best chance for success. (Government of Canada, 2019, What is a business plan and why do I need one?)

© Peshkova/Shutterstock.com

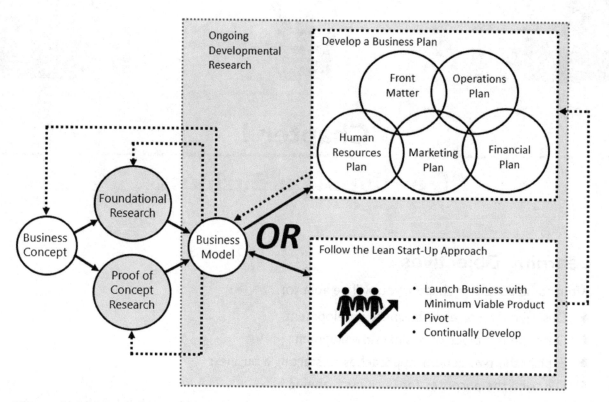

Figure I.   Business Plan or Lean Start Up

(Illustration by Lee A. Swanson)

This chapter describes the stages of business development, types of business development (Figure 1), and the purposes, principles, general concepts, and tools for business planning. It also describes the process for developing a business plan.

Business Development Stages

Generally, entrepreneurship is considered to consist of the following elements (Brooks, 2009; Mitchell, 2000):

Searching and Ideation

The searching phase, also called idea formulation or opportunity recognition, begins when a person decides they might want to be an entrepreneur, or when an existing entrepreneur decides they need more ideas in their idea pool. It involves purposefully developing business ideas, often through a process called ideation (Kier & McMullen, 2018). The phase ends when there are a sufficient number of ideas in the idea pool.

The number of ideas required depends on their likely viability, along with other factors

like the entrepreneur's skill sets and interests. Entrepreneurs should strive to have at least three or four viable ideas in their idea pool to screen and from which to choose one to pursue. Some experts suggest that entrepreneurs should maintain an idea pool from which to consider new venture ideas and expansions to existing ventures (Mitchell, 2000).

Idea Screening

The idea screening phase, or concept development, begins when the person with the idea pool is no longer focusing on adding new ideas to it; but is instead taking steps to choose the best idea based on specific criteria. This phase ends when the entrepreneur chooses one idea from among those in the idea pool.

© 13_Phunkod/Shutterstock.com

Creative problem solving through *ideation*, and the related concept of *new venture ideation*, which is "the generation and selection of ideas for the creation of a new venture" (Kier & McMullen, 2018, p. 2267), can help entrepreneurs search for and screen ideas.

Planning and Financing

The planning and financing phase begins when idea screening ends and the entrepreneur begins making plans to implement the single idea chosen from the idea pool and secures the financing needed to support the venture idea. This phase ends when sufficient business planning has been done and when adequate financing has been arranged.

© Have a nice day Photo/Shutterstock.com

This book focuses on the planning element of this stage of business development. We briefly discuss the lean start up approach as a form of business planning, but most of this book is about the actual business planning process. The concepts in this book can be applied to business planning for a new venture, but also for businesses in the ongoing operations phase described later.

Set Up

The set up phase begins after the planning and financing stage ends, and the person begins implementing the plans needed to start the business. This phase ends when the business is ready to launch.

The set up process involves the many actions an entrepreneur needs to take to prepare for start up. Those actions include purchasing and installing equipment, securing the venture location, finishing all the needed renovations, recruiting and hiring staff, acquiring business licenses, purchasing the initial inventory, incurring the preopening advertising costs, buying the various types of insurance needed by the business, incorporating the business, and making sure that the business systems required for start up are in place.

Business plans for new ventures must describe the research into, and the plans made by the entrepreneurs to set up their businesses.

Start Up

The start up phase begins after set up is complete, and the business opens and begins making sales. The phase ends when the business has moved beyond the point where the entrepreneur must continually fight for the business's survival and persistence. It ends when the entrepreneur can instead shift emphasis toward business growth or maintaining the venture's stability.

Almost all business plans for new ventures will cover the start up phase

over the first few years of planned operations and projected financial results. The activities that occur during this phase begin from about the time that the first sales are expected. The business plan will include the costs for activities like planned grand opening events and must reflect expected sales fluctuations. Those fluctuations might reflect early adopter purchases followed by possible lulls in sales while the business becomes more established and builds up its customer base until more regular and steady sales patterns evolve when the start up phase (which might last for three or four years) ends, and ongoing operations begin.

Entrepreneurs writing business plans for new ventures must fully describe the plans they have for starting up their business along with their financial projections from the time they will begin spending and earning money to a few years into the future.

Ongoing Operations

The ongoing operations phase begins when the start up phase ends, and the business shifts its focus from survival to growth (or maintenance) strategies. The phase ends when the entrepreneur chooses to exit from the business and harvest the value they generated with the venture.

When writing business plans for new ventures, entrepreneurs must describe how they plan to operate their business to prove to their targeted business plan readers that the business will eventually move beyond the start up phase and become a viable ongoing business.

© Odua Images/Shutterstock.com

© Castleski/Shutterstock.com

In some cases, entrepreneurs might write business plans for ventures that are in the ongoing operations phase and are looking to expand, change their business model, or prepare for business succession or other forms of exit.

Exit

When entrepreneurs decide to sell or transfer ownership of their business or implement measures that allow their company to run without their direct involvement, they exit their business. These can also be called harvest methods. As any chosen exit strategy will have significant implications on the decisions an entrepreneur makes regarding almost all other aspects of their business, it is vital to determine the exit strategy early.

When considering an exit from a business through a transfer to other people—like family members or existing employees—an entrepreneur should have a good succession plan in place to help make the transfer go smoothly. Sometimes, a business plan is needed to chart the pathway toward business succession.

© Gordoenkoff/Shutterstock.com

© fizkes/Shutterstock.com

Types of Business Development

Both venture start ups and businesses in the ongoing operations phase implement business development plans. Start up business development involves implementing plans to convert a business idea into a viable ongoing venture. Ongoing businesses that implement development plans do so for a variety of reasons, including to facilitate growth, respond to new market realities, and for business succession (passing leadership or ownership to a successor, facilitating a management or employee purchase, or selling the business to someone else).

The business plan development process described throughout this book applies to both new business start ups and to planning for business expansions and succession.

Two General Approaches to Starting a Business

As shown in Figure 1, after entrepreneurs develop a business concept, they should conduct proof of concept research to answer questions about the viability of the business idea along with some foundational research to get answers to important questions like what general time, effort, and expenses must they incur to start such a business. The answers they get should help them develop a business model. They should continue to seek answers about the likely viability of the business idea as defined by the business model, and make changes to the idea and the associated business model until they believe they are viable. Entrepreneurs can then take one of two general approaches to potentially launch the business.

If the entrepreneur has a *minimum viable product* available to take to market and continually and rapidly adapt based on feedback from the market, they may be able to launch their business using the lean start up approach (Ries, 2011). Alternatively, if the business model calls for a relatively extensive set up phase, potentially including the development of a facility before being able to begin making sales, or if financing will be required to start the business, the entrepreneur might need to develop a business plan.

The following section briefly describes the lean start up approach. The remainder of this chapter covers the business plan development process expanded upon throughout the rest of this book.

Lean Start Up

Ries (2011) defines a lean start up as "a human institution designed to create a new product or service under conditions of extreme uncertainty" (p. 27). The lean start up approach involves releasing a *minimal viable product* to customers with the expectation that this early prototype will change and evolve frequently and quickly in response to customer feedback. This is meant to be a relatively easy and inexpensive way to develop a product or service by relying on customer feedback to guide

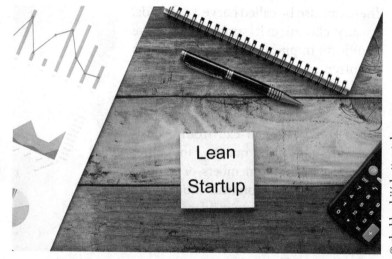

© chubbychii/shutterstokc.com

the *pivots* in new directions that will ultimately—and relatively quickly—lead to a product or service with the appeal required for business success. It is only then that the actual business will emerge. As such, entrepreneurs who apply the lean start up approach—because their business idea allows for it—actually forgo developing a business plan, at least until they might need one later to get financing, because introducing a *minimum viable product* helps "entrepreneurs start the process of learning as quickly as possible" (Ries, 2011, p. 93). This is followed by ever-improving versions of their products or services. However, all entrepreneurs must directly consult with their potential target purchasers and end users to assess whether and how the market might respond to their proposed venture. The proof of concept research and foundational research activities should include purposeful and meaningful interactions between the entrepreneur and the target purchasers and end users.

Ries's (2011) five lean start up principles start with the idea that entrepreneurs are everywhere and that anyone working in an environment where they seek to create new products or services "under conditions of extreme uncertainty" (p. 27) can use the lean start up approach. Second, a start up is more than the product or service: it is an institution that must be managed in a new way that promotes growth through innovation. Third, start ups are about learning "how to build a sustainable business" (p. 8–9) by validating product or service design through frequent prototyping that allows entrepreneurs to test the concepts. Forth, start ups must follow this process or feedback loop: create products and services; measure how the market reacts to them; and learn from that to determine whether to pivot or to persevere with an outcome the market accepts. Finally, Ries (2011) suggested that entrepreneurial outcomes and innovation initiatives need to be measured through innovative accounting.

Business Planning

While the lean start up approach works well for many types of businesses. Entrepreneurs wishing to launch ventures that require significant up-front funding or lengthy and expensive time lines to get to the stage where they can begin delivering a product—a minimum viable product or otherwise—usually have to develop business plans.

© takasu/Shutterstock.com

Purposes for Developing Business Plans

Business plans are developed for both internal and external purposes. Internally, entrepreneurs develop business plans to help put the pieces of their business together. Externally, the most common purpose is to raise capital.

Internal Purposes

As the road map for a business's development, the business plan

- Defines the vision for the company
- Establishes the company's strategy
- Describes how the strategy will be implemented
- Provides a framework for the analysis of key issues
- Provides a plan for the development of the business
- Helps the entrepreneur develop and measure critical success factors
- Helps the entrepreneur to be realistic and test theories

External Purposes

A well–written business plan can help an entrepreneur calculate a possible value for their business concept. Thus, it is often the primary tool for describing a company to external audiences while backing up a claim as to its valuation. A good business plan can help outside parties understand the current status of the company, its opportunities, and its needs for resources such as capital and personnel.

Communications and Credibility in a Business Plan

Hindle and Mainprize (2006) suggested that business plan writers must strive to effectively communicate their expectations about the nature of an uncertain future and to project credibility. The *liabilities of newness* make communicating the expected future of new ventures much more complicated than for existing businesses. Consequently, business plan writers should adhere to five specific *communication principles*. First, business plans must be written to meet the *expectations* of targeted readers in terms of what they need to know to support the proposed business. They should also lay out the *milestones* that investors or other targeted readers need to know. Finally, writers must clearly outline the *opportunity*, the *context* within the proposed venture will operate (internal and external environment), and the *business model* (Hindle & Mainprize, 2006).

There are also five *business plan credibility principles* that writers should consider; the team, elaborate plans, integrate scenarios, financial links, and the deal. Business plan writers should build and establish their credibility by highlighting essential and relevant information about the venture *team*. Writers need to *elaborate* on the plans they outline in

© garagestock/Shutterstock.com

© Jirsak/Shutterstock.com

their document so that targeted readers have the information they need to assess the plan's credibility. To build and establish credibility, they must *integrate scenarios* to show that the entrepreneur has made realistic assumptions and has adequately anticipated what the future holds for their proposed venture. Writers need to provide comprehensive and realistic *financial links* between all relevant components of the plan. Finally, they must outline *the deal* or the value that targeted readers should expect to derive from their involvement with the venture (Hindle & Mainprize, 2006).

Establishing and Maintaining Credibility

Targeted business plan readers automatically discount anything they read in a plan that is not backed up with a valid source. Business plan writers must convince readers that the information in the plan is valid by backing everything up with a relevant source or by first convincing the reader that the entrepreneur has the knowledge or experience necessary to make the claims shown in the plan. If the writer fails to convince targeted readers that everything included in the plan came from a valid source, readers are likely to discount the work and behave in undesirable ways, like rejecting the opportunity to invest in the business.

One of the best ways to establish and maintain credibility is to back up or support every claim made in the business plan. A business plan writer must cite all sources of information for ethical reasons, but doing so also helps build their credibility (or helps avoid destroying it). A practical reason to properly reference the work is that targeted business plan readers often look up some of the references used.

To establish and build a business plan writer's credibility, and that of the information they include in the plan, they should use a formal referencing method like APA.

Refer to the following examples of references to different kinds of sources business plan writers might use to establish their credibility and that of their plan. The following examples use APA referencing methods.

1. Business plan writers should reference reports written by acknowledged researchers or research agencies.

   For example, if a writer used the following industry report from the IBISWorld database written by S. Morea, they would cite the work in-text - for example, (Morea, 2018). If they used the following report without an identified author from the Conference Board of Canada for an economic forecast for the United States, they would cite it using the organisation's name - for example, (Conference Board of Canada, 2019). The following references would appear in the business plan's reference list.

   Conference Board of Canada. (2019). *Monthly economic series report: Posted June 12, 2019.* Retrieved from https://www.conferenceboard.ca

   Morea, S. (2018). *Auto parts wholesaling in Canada. (IBISWorld Industry Report 41529CA).* Retrieved from http://www.ibisworld.com

2. Business plan writers often reference online catalogues from industrial suppliers to get prices (usually including taxes) for items the company must purchase during set up, like office furniture and machines.

   For example, if the writer got the after-tax price of $986 to purchase three industrial quality fire extinguishers from the following source, they would cite the source in-text - for example, (Uline, 2019) and add the following to the reference list.

   Uline. (2019). Fire extinguishers. Retrieved from https://www.uline.ca/BL_990/Fire-Extinguishers

3. Business plan writers will usually get quotes from sources like insurance brokers. If, for example, a writer received an insurance quote from Ms. Amil Franksen from ABC Insurance Company detailing the cost to purchase business insurance, they would include an in-text citation in their business plan - for example, (A. Franksen, personal communication, June 15, 2019). They would not include a corresponding entry in the reference list because the quote received would not be a published document that others could access.

4. Similar to the previous example, if the business plan writer met with and received expert advice from someone named Sahil Sharma who ran a similar business, they would use an in-text citation - for example (S. Sharma, personal communication, May 16, 2019), but would not include a reference list item because the information would not be available for anyone else to find.

The Ratchet Effect

A ratchet is a tool with which most of us are familiar. It is useful because it helps its user accomplish something while protecting against the loss of past advancements. A business plan writer should accomplish two important things with each word, sentence, paragraph, heading, chart, figure, and table they include in a plan. First, everything they include should be needed and relevant. Second, everything they add to the plan should build their credibility as the entrepreneur and the credibility of their plan.

Business plan writers should apply the ratchet effect by making sure that every sentence and paragraph conveys needed and relevant information that builds credibility. They should apply the ratchet effect by doing the following:

- Business plan writers should rarely repeat anything they include in their plan.
- Business plan writers should avoid using *killer phrases*, like "there is no competition for our product" and "our product will sell itself, so we will not need to advertise it." Savvy readers will understand that these kinds of statements are naive and demonstrate a lack of understanding about how the market and other real-life factors work.
- Business plan writers should avoid including contradictory statements in their plan. They must make sure that the contents in all of the written parts align, and that the statements in the written parts line up with the contents of the financial parts.

Context and Framing

Business plan writers must provide the right context when describing situations, strategies, and other components of a plan. Business plan readers should never be left to guess why something is included in a plan. Proper context is needed to help frame the information presented.

One example of effective framing is when the business plan writer indicates how the entrepreneur's education, expertise, relevant experiences, and network of contacts will make up for any lack of direct experience they have in running a particular kind of business. An example of ineffective framing is when the writer indicates that the entrepreneur lacks experience with this type of business, or when they fail to specify how and why the entrepreneur's levels of experience will affect the business's development.

General Guidelines for Developing Business Plans

Many businesses must have a business plan to achieve their goals. Using a standard format helps the reader understand that the entrepreneur has thought everything through and that the returns justify the risk. The following are some basic guidelines for business plan development.

- If appropriate, include catchy, professional graphics on the title page to make it appealing to targeted readers, but do not go overboard.
- If targeted readers will receive a hard copy of the business plan, bind it so it will not fall apart. Use a three-ring binder, coil binding, or a similar method to keep the pages together in the right order. Make sure the binding method used does not obscure the information next to where it is bound.
- Make sure to order and number all of the pages correctly.
- Number all major sections and subsections within the plan using the format shown in the Word template (Appendix B).
- Use the styles and references features in Word to automatically number and format the section titles and to generate the table of contents. To ensure that all the numbering will be correct,

update the automatic numbering and automatically generated tables just before printing the plan.

- Before submitting the plan, be sure to meet all of the following requirements:
  - Completely integrate everything contained in the business plan. The written part must say the same thing as the financial part.
  - Meet all financial statements requirements, including making sure that the balance sheets balance.
  - Make sure that everything is correct. There should be no spelling, grammar, sentence structure, referencing, or calculation errors.
  - Ensure that the document is well organized and formatted. Apply a layout that makes the document easy to read and comprehend. Locate all diagrams, charts, statements, and other additions in the parts of the plan best suited to them, and make sure that they are easy to find.
  - When it strengthens the plan to do so, show some information in both text and table or figure formats. However, avoid repetition as it is usually unnecessary to state the same thing more than once.
- Include all the information necessary to enable readers to understand everything in the business plan.
- Use clear and consistent terms in the business plan. For example, avoid using confusing statements like the following:

"There is a shortage of 100,000 units with competitors currently producing 25,000. We can help fill this huge gap in demand with our capacity to produce 5,000 units."

This statement might mean there is a total shortage of 100,000 units, but competitors are filling this gap by producing 25,000 per year; in which case, there will only be a shortage for four years. However, it could also mean that the annual shortage is 100,000 units and only 25,000 are produced each year, in which case the total shortage is very high and is growing each year.

- Always provide a complete perspective by indicating the appropriate time frame, currency, or size.
- When including a percentage figure, always indicate what the number is a percentage of; otherwise, the number is meaningless to a reader.
- If the business plan includes an international element, indicate in which currency or currencies the costs, revenues, prices, or other values are quoted. When a business operation includes more than one currency, the business plan should acknowledge the exchange rate risk and describe how it will be mitigated.
- If a statement presents something as a fact when this fact is not generally known, always indicate the source. Unsupported statements damage credibility.
- Be specific. A business plan loses value if it uses vague references to things like high demand and carefully set prices. When possible, include actual and properly referenced numbers, prices, and real data acquired through proper research. In some cases, realistic assumptions might be required.
- Integrate all of the strategies described in the plan. For example, a pricing strategy must complement and mesh perfectly with the product or service strategy, distribution strategy, and promotions strategy. If the business provides a premium product, it should typically also charge a premium price.
- Before finalizing the business plan, reread each section to evaluate whether it will appeal to targeted readers.

Process for Developing Business Plans

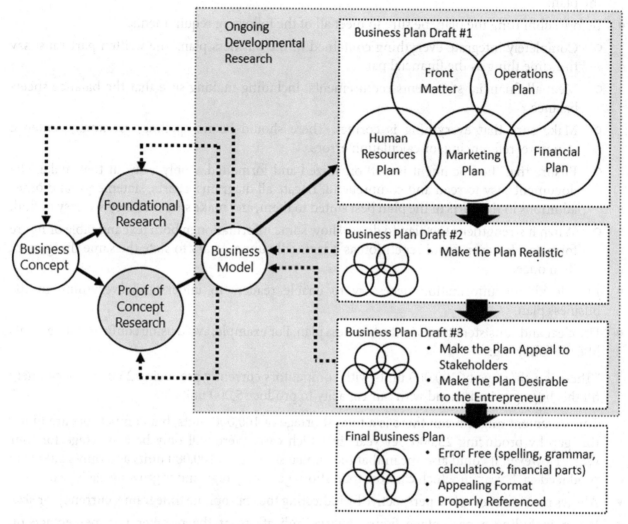

Figure 2. Process for Developing Business Plans

(Illustration by Lee A. Swanson)

The Business Concept

As shown in Figure 2, entrepreneurs interested in starting a new business must first have a business concept.

For information on developing a business concept, review the "Searching and Ideation" section of this chapter and complete Exercise 1.1.

Proof of Concept Research

As shown in Figure 2, proof of concept research supports the development and

continual adaptations to the business model to make it more realistic, appealing to investors, and desirable for the entrepreneur.

Proof of concept research addresses the following question:

> Can the business concept be converted into a viable and sustainable business entity?

Entrepreneurs and investors—and potentially other stakeholders, like targeted employees and needed suppliers—require an affirmative answer to this question before they will be willing to develop the concept into a business. However, not all "yes" answers are sufficient to lead to a decision to start the business. The stronger the "yes" to this question, the more likely it is that the entrepreneur will choose to start the business.

Refer to Chapter 2 for information on conducting proof of concept research and use *Appendix A* to help guide research efforts.

Foundational Research

The feedback loops in Figure 2 indicate that foundational research supports business model development and continual adaptation.

Foundational research seeks to answer the following question:

> From a general perspective, what resources—including time, knowledge, people, money, equipment, and facilities—and investment are required to convert the business concept into a viable and sustainable business entity?

In addition to conducting the research required to confirm that a business concept can become a viable and ongoing business, entrepreneurs need to know what resources are required to start the business. The purpose of foundational research is to provide the entrepreneur with a general—yet as accurate as possible—idea of the time and money that will be needed to launch the business. To figure this out, the entrepreneur must also determine what assets and human resources the business will require to start.

Refer to Chapter 2 for a discussion on the types of information foundational research should uncover for entrepreneurs. Use *Appendix A* to help guide your research efforts.

Ongoing Developmental Research

Figure 2 shows that ongoing developmental research is less concerned with developing the business model than are proof of concept and foundational research. However, ongoing developmental research—which occurs until the third draft of the business plan is complete, and the plan is realistic, appealing to investors, and desirable for the entrepreneur—might uncover new information indicating that the entrepreneur needs to adapt the business model.

Ongoing developmental research seeks to get increasingly accurate answers to the following question:

Entrepreneurs must conduct ongoing research into what purchases, actions, partnerships, and other things are needed to launch the business and sustain it. Ongoing developmental research includes the

> From a detailed perspective, what resources and investment are required to efficiently and effectively set up, start up, and sustain ongoing business operations?

research entrepreneurs need to do to figure out everything that needs to be purchased and done—along with all of the associated costs—to get the business going and maintain it. The answers they get should help them develop their business plan and alert them to needed adaptations to the business model.

Read Chapter 2 for information on conducting ongoing developmental research and use *Appendix A* to support your research.

The Business Model

Inherent in any business plan is a description of the *business model* chosen by the entrepreneur as the one that they feel will best ensure success. Through research, entrepreneurs should determine how each element of their business model—including their revenue streams, cost structure, customer segments, value propositions, key activities, key partners, key resources, customer relationships, and channels—can fit together to improve the potential success of their business venture (see Chapter 3).

Some business models can be operationalized by launching a lean start up and growing their business by continually pivoting, or adjusting their business model in response to the real-time signals they get from the markets' reactions to their business operations.

In other cases, entrepreneurs will require business plans to operationalize their business models. In those cases, their initial business model will provide the basis for that plan. Of course, throughout this and all stages in this process, the entrepreneur should seek to continually gather information and adjust the plans in response to the new knowledge they gather by conducting their research.

As shown by the feedback loops in Figure 2, the entrepreneur will continually conduct proof of concept, foundational, and ongoing developmental research, and use the results from that research to persistently adjust the business model to make it ever more viable.

Refer to Chapter 3 for information on business models.

First Business Plan Draft

Entrepreneurs should write a first draft of their business plan that includes the results from their research and explains their business model (in a business plan format). Many entrepreneurs prefer to create a full draft of the business plan with all of the sections, including the front part with the business description, vision, mission, values, value proposition statement, preliminary set of goals, and possibly even a table of contents and lists of tables and figures all set up using the software features enabling their automatic generation. Writing all of the operations, human resources, marketing, and financial plans as part of the first draft ensures that all of these parts can be appropriately and necessarily integrated. The business plan will tell the story of a planned business start up in two ways: (a) through words, charts, and graphs in the operations, human resources, and marketing plans and (b) through the financial plan. Both must tell the same story.

Use Chapters 4 to 8 for guidance on developing the first business plan draft.

Making Business Plan Realistic

The first draft of a business plan will rarely be realistic. As the entrepreneur writes the plan, it will necessarily change as new information is acquired. Another factor that usually renders the first draft unrealistic is the difficulty in making sure that the written part—in the front part of the plan along with the operations, human resources, and marketing plans—tells the same story as the financial part does. This stage of work involves making the necessary adjustments to the plan to make it as realistic as possible.

As shown in Figure 2 by the feedback loop from the second business plan draft to the business model, in order to make the business plan realistic, the entrepreneur might need to change the business model. If they change it, they will likely need to change some critical elements of their initial business plan draft, especially if the business model changes were relatively significant.

As indicated in Figure 2, ongoing developmental research should be conducted throughout the business planning process. The entrepreneur will need to conduct this ongoing research and make needed adjustments to the draft business plan until the plan is realistic. They then need to conduct further research and make new adjustments until the business plan is appealing to stakeholders and desirable to the entrepreneur.

Refer to Chapter 9 for information on making the business plan draft realistic.

Making Plan Appeal to Stakeholders and Desirable to the Entrepreneur

A business plan can be realistic without appealing to potential investors and other external stakeholders, like employees, suppliers, and needed business partners. In this case, the external stakeholders will not behave as the entrepreneur wants by investing in the business, and possibly also by avoiding considering the new business as a viable employer, a reliable customer to which to supply the product, and a dependable business partner. In short, a business plan is not useful until it is appealing to targeted investors and other stakeholders.

A business plan might be realistic and appeal to stakeholders without being desirable to the entrepreneur. The business planning process might indicate that the business will not generate enough profit for the entrepreneur to thrive. It might also uncover other potential issues for the entrepreneur, like showing that they will have to work too many hours or will have to pledge too many personal assets to secure needed loans. In this case, the entrepreneur will not—or should not—move forward with starting the business.

After the business plan is realistic, the entrepreneur must continue to develop the business model and the business plan—while retaining the realism—until the plan indicates that it will appeal to stakeholders, and presents a desirable business venture for the entrepreneur. The plan might need relatively extensive adjustments to show a viable exit strategy and adequate expected returns on investment for potential investors. The business plan must also convince potential investors that the entrepreneur can accomplish all that they promised in the plan. For the entrepreneur, the plan needs to show that they can get what they want out of the business to make it worthwhile for them to start and run it.

The caution at this stage is to balance the need to make realistic plans that are desirable to investors with the need to meet the entrepreneur's goals without the entrepreneur becoming discouraged enough to drop the idea of pursuing the business idea. If an entrepreneur is convinced that the proposed venture will satisfy a market need, there is often a way to assemble the financing required and operate the business while also meeting the entrepreneur's most important goals. To do so, however, might require significant changes to the business model driven by a superior understanding of what targeted investors need from a business proposal before they invest.

Chapter 10 describes how to make a business plan appealing and desirable.

Finishing the Business Plan

The final stage of the process, as shown in Figure 2, involves putting the essential finishing touches on the business plan so that it will present well to potential investors and others. This involves making sure that the calculations and links between the written and financial parts are accurate. It involves making all the needed corrections to the spelling, grammar, and formatting. The final set of goals should be written to appeal to the target readers and to reflect what the business plan says. The final step is to write a robust executive summary that will make potential investors want to consider investing in the venture.

For information on finishing the business plan, refer to Chapter 11.

Business Plan Worksheets and Templates

Included with this book are three tools, along with a cross-chapter case, to help business plan writers develop comprehensive business plans. To develop a full and comprehensive business plan, users should use the following items in concert:

- The contents of this book along with the end–of–chapter exercises and cross-chapter case
- Research Analyses Worksheets
- Business Plan Word Template
- Business Plan Excel Template

Chapters 4 to 11 in this book cover the information required for each element within the Business Plan Templates.

Chapter Summary

This chapter described the stages of business development and the types of business development followed by descriptions of the two general approaches to starting a business plan; using the lean start up approach and developing a business plan to use as a guide to starting the business and to use when seeking funding. The chapter covered the internal and external purposes for business planning. It also explained how business plans must effectively communicate while establishing and building credibility for both the entrepreneur and the venture. The general guidelines for business planning were covered, as was the process for developing business plans.

Exercises

Exercise 1.1—Ideation

Apply some of the ideation tools and techniques described and provided through the following sites to develop and test new venture ideas:

1. Board of Innovation: https://www.boardofinnovation.com/staff_picks/our-favorite-ideation-tools/.
2. HubSpot: https://blog.hubspot.com/marketing/creative-exercises-better-than-brainstorming.
3. Entrepreneur.com: https://www.entrepreneur.com/article/287568.
4. IDEO U: https://www.ideou.com/pages/ideation-method-mash-up.
5. Stanford: https://dschool.stanford.edu/resources.

Exercise 1.2—Getting a Start with the Business Plan Word and Excel Templates

1. Review the business plan Word template provided with this book (Appendix B). Note how the sections of this book are referenced throughout the template.
2. Load the financial model Excel template provided with this book (Appendix C). Scroll through each of the worksheets contained in the template. Note how some cells in the worksheets are shaded in blue, indicating that they are input cells. As numbers are added to those input cells, relevant numbers are transferred to other worksheets, including the financial statements worksheets. A business plan writer can develop an entire financial model that generates complete financial statements by entering numbers only in the blue input cells.

Cross-Chapter Case—Tech World Pro Part 1

The Story Begins

Talia and Malik Garcia had discussed starting a business together since the day they met while she was in her final year of business school and Malik was two years from finishing his education degree. Since then, they married, finished their college education, gained some experience in the workforce, and had a son named Owen, now 3 years old.

After graduating, Talia worked for a bank for three years before starting her maternity leave. She returned to work six months ago. Malik has been a high school mathematics teacher for about three years. Now, more than ever, the couple wants to start a business.

They live in a beautiful suburban area of their city not far from their parents. Talia's mother and father own and operate a restaurant and Malik's parents expect to retire from their teaching and accounting careers in about 10 years. Both sets of parents are financially secure and have offered to support the couple when they start their business. Talia's uncle and aunt, who own a chain of clothing stores and like to invest in commercial real estate, also expressed their interest in helping the couple with their entrepreneurial endeavors. Additionally, Talia and Malik have $78,000 in savings, much of which came from an inheritance.

Other than having a general interest in owning a retail store, Talia and Malik are not yet sure what kind of business to start. They love all outdoor activities, including hiking and kayaking in the nearby forest and lake region, have a new interest in children's clothing and toys because of Owen, and are accomplished but amateur musicians who also like electronics, judging by the audio and computer equipment they have accumulated.

Cross-Chapter Case Activities—Part 1

1. Based on the information in this chapter, discuss how Talia and Malik should proceed with their goal to start a business.

© dotshock/Shutterstock.com

Chapter 2

Proof of Concept Research, Foundational Research, and Ongoing Developmental Research

Learning Objectives

After completing this chapter, you will be able to:

◆ Describe and contrast the purposes for proof of concept, foundational, and ongoing developmental research

◆ Apply methods for conducting proof of concept, foundational, and ongoing developmental research

◆ Conduct useful research while considering the various levels of analysis and while applying the appropriate analysis tools for each level

Overview

All information presented in a business plan as being factual should be backed up with valid primary or secondary sources. In some cases, entrepreneurs can first establish their credentials—based on their education, experience, and expertise—and claim that those credentials qualify them to state information as being factual. In both cases, evidence-based claims make the business plan stronger.

© Rawpixel.com/Shutterstock.com

This chapter introduces the distinct types of research used to support business plan development; proof of concept, foundational, and ongoing developmental research (Figure 3). It also covers the levels of analyses that must be considered and stresses the importance of applying the appropriate tools to conduct the analyses at each level (Figure 8).

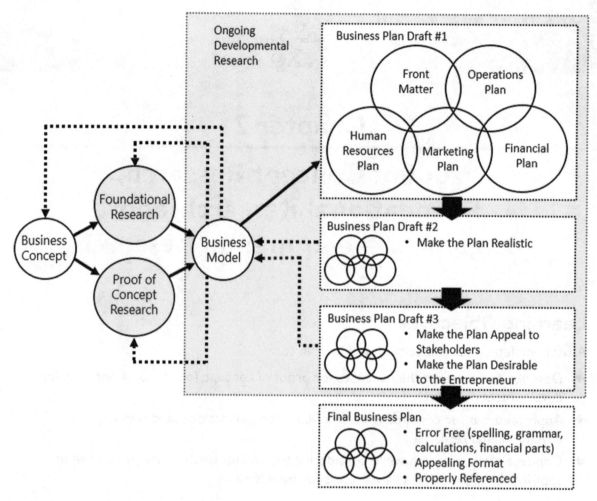

Figure 3.   Three Types of Research

(Illustration by Lee A. Swanson)

Research Analyses Worksheets

Refer to *Appendix A* for a tool to help business plan writers conduct useful research. Note that the tool follows a *key-questions-first* approach to conducting research.

Conducting the Three Types of Business Plan Research

© Jirapong Manustrong/Shutterstock.com

Be aware that there will be overlaps between the three types of business plan research; proof of concept, foundational, and ongoing developmental research (see Figure 4).

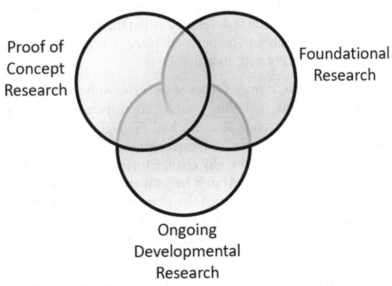

Figure 4. Three Types of Business Plan Research

(Illustration by Lee A. Swanson)

The three types of research each have a distinct purpose as described later, but, in practice, there is sometimes no clear distinction between the types of research. For example, when meeting with people who have started and run businesses like the kind the entrepreneur is starting, the entrepreneur is likely to gather information to help them prove that the business can be viable (proof of concept research), that will help them develop and back up strategies (foundational research), and that will give them insight into the costs they will incur (ongoing developmental research).

Proof of Concept Research Purpose, Key Questions, and Methods

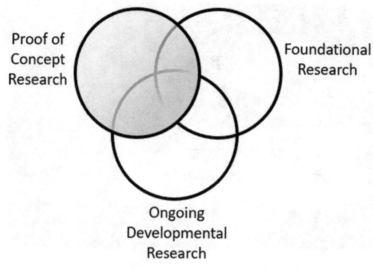

Figure 5.   Proof of Concept Research

(Illustration by Lee A. Swanson)

Purpose

The purpose for *proof of concept research* (see Figure 5) is to prove—as much as possible, and with increasing relevance and impact as the plan is developed—that the business is likely to succeed using the business model described throughout the business plan. It primarily supports business plan development by focusing on its viability and sustainability.

For a business to succeed and persist, it must be based on a robust business model with a carefully crafted set of business model elements, including a value proposition that addresses a market need, a viable cost structure, appropriate revenue streams, and the right customer segments (for more information on business models, see Chapter 3). Developing a viable business model is an iterative process by which an entrepreneur will continually change their business model—or pivot—as they gather new information. Proof of concept research helps them test business model concepts until they eventually settle on one upon which to launch their business. After starting the business, smart entrepreneurs will continually adjust the elements of their business model—based on research, often in the form of testing new approaches to see how they work—to ensure that their business becomes and remains viable.

Compelling proof of concept research outcomes should help the entrepreneur develop a viable business model *and* convince the entrepreneur and targeted investors that it is worthwhile for them to invest their resources in a business founded on the business model.

Key Questions

To effectively conduct and present proof of concept research, a business plan writer must anticipate what information potential investors will require before they will be convinced that the business idea is viable enough that they should risk their money by investing in that venture. To do this, the entrepreneur should imagine that they are considering risking their money on the idea (which they likely are) and list as many questions as possible to which they would require answers. That list is likely to include questions like the following.

- What other solutions are there that deliver similar results? How much do they cost relative to this idea? What are the advantages and disadvantages of each possible solution, of which this idea is one?
- How many potential customers are there? How much is each potential customer likely to buy?
- What would it take for a company to replace what they do now with this solution? Would they need to take measures like replacing existing people or equipment, and what other challenges do they face in adopting this solution?
- What specific value proposition elements—perhaps like reductions in operating costs, reduced risk of injuries, and increased accuracy and reliability of operating processes—does the entrepreneur need to prove to potential investors, and what type of proof is needed (e.g., reasonable cost reduction estimates, estimates of gained employee workdays due to reduced injuries, and estimated revenue increases due to improvements in operating processes).

Methods

Proof of concept research is best conducted by directly asking targeted customers, suppliers, and others about their perspectives, intentions, needs, challenges, and other things for which the proposed business might provide solutions. Conducting this type of primary research will help the entrepreneur learn whether their current business model concept might generate enough revenue to cover the projected expenses and make the business viable and sustainable.

In some cases, secondary research can validate the need for a business and provide evidence that a particular business model might support a viable and sustainable business. This is usually the case when others have conducted research that concludes that a particular business is needed and is likely to be successful in a particular location.

Foundational Research Purpose, Key Questions, and Methods

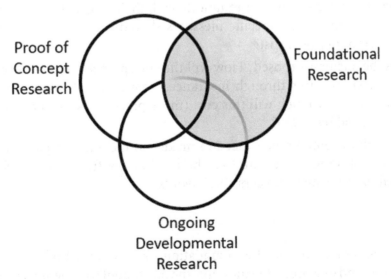

Figure 6. Foundational Research

(Illustration by Lee A. Swanson)

Purpose

Foundational research (see Figure 6) is conducted to develop and back up the plans and strategies that comprise the business model and form much of the business plan.

Foundational research, like proof of concept research, is not something that can be initiated and completed within a few hours or days. Foundational research needs to be conducted as the business model is continually adapted throughout the business plan development process, and as new information is needed for the business model and the business plan to develop and support strategies.

Effective foundational research outcomes should provide the entrepreneur with the knowledge needed to launch the business and sustain it with practical strategies and tactics *and* convince the entrepreneur and targeted investors that they should invest their resources in the business.

Key Questions

The questions business plan writers should use to guide their foundational research include those needed to develop and support strategies across all sections of the business plan. Some relevant questions might include the following.

- What fixed assets, including equipment and machinery, must be purchased before this business can start? How much does the entrepreneur expect all of this to cost (more precise costs can be determined through ongoing developmental research)? How long will it take to order, install, test, and make sure that the equipment and machinery will work as needed (before start up)?

- What are the average salaries and wages for the categories of employees in the industry for the geographic region?

- What is the optimum mix of pricing, distribution, promotions, and product decisions to best appeal to how the targeted customers make their buying decisions?

- Does the entrepreneur need to be concerned mainly with their direct competitors, or does this kind of business also need to worry about customers choosing to spend their money on indirect competitors' products and services instead of the proposed business's products or services?

- In what ways will the entrepreneur communicate with their targeted customers? When will they communicate with them? What specific messages should they plan to convey to them? How much will this promotions plan cost?

- To what risks is the business exposed? How will the entrepreneur mitigate each of the identified risks? When transferring risks through insurance, what kinds of insurance does the business need to purchase and how much will this cost (more precise costs can be determined through ongoing developmental research)?

- What decisions will the entrepreneur need to make and include in a partnership agreement or articles of incorporation to make sure that the business partners account for all of the likely scenarios related to ownership transfers and buyouts?

Methods

Like with proof of concept research, the best foundational research method is to meet with someone who has already started and operated a business like the one the entrepreneur wishes to start. Not only might it be possible to get essential answers to important questions from such a person, that person might also provide essential information that the entrepreneur did not know they needed. Most often, the real value an entrepreneur gains from conducting foundational research by interviewing experts is the information they gain that they did not know they needed.

Entrepreneurs must also conduct a significant amount of secondary research as part of their foundational research approach. In all cases, they must use acknowledged, valid sources for the information they use in a business plan.

One example of when business plan writers need to use secondary research is when they need to determine how much to inflate projected costs from one year to another in their financial models. They should first determine which categories of costs should be inflated by which *projected price index*. Some cost categories might be inflated using projected consumer price indices from recognized and valid sources like Conference Board of Canada, United States Congressional Budget Office, and the Organisation for Economic Co-operation and Development (OECD). Other cost categories should be inflated using other measures like projected gross domestic product (GDP) growth, producer price index (PPI), and industry measures like those that might be found through industry associations that project industry-specific costs.

In some cases, entrepreneurs should use *proxies* to project costs. For example, when trying to figure out how much they will have to pay for a facility, business plan writers should consider that any retail, commercial, or industrial space currently listed on commercial real estate sites might not be available when they are ready to secure a location. In those cases, they can select one or more currently listed properties to use as proxies for the space they hope to secure in the future. They might select a listing of a space like that they need to secure in the area in which they hope to locate so they can determine things like how much the property taxes will be if they intend to purchase a property, or how much the lease costs will be. If no property is currently listed that meets the entrepreneur's needs, they can look at a listing for a similar sized property in the desired area to determine some costs and another property elsewhere to figure out costs for things like building renovations.

Ongoing Developmental Research Purpose, Key Questions, and Methods

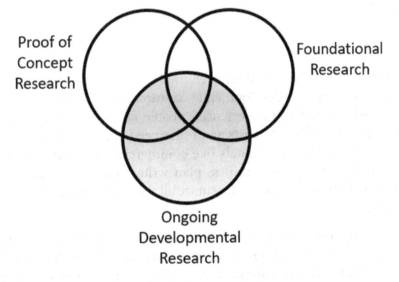

Figure 7. Ongoing Developmental Research

(Illustration by Lee A. Swanson)

Purpose

Ongoing developmental research (see Figure 7) is used to back up the facts presented in the business plan and to calculate things like the costs of developing the business.

Effective ongoing developmental research outcomes should help the entrepreneur finalize a business plan that includes actual costs, realistic revenue projections, the details about the insurance options and other risk mitigation methods the company should use, and other information needed to convey the viability of the venture. With useful ongoing developmental research backed up by good references, the entrepreneur and targeted investors should feel confident about investing their resources in the business. Although focused more on generating the information needed to develop the business plan, ongoing developmental research outcomes will help the entrepreneur make necessary adaptations to the business model.

Key Questions

The following are examples of the types of questions business plan writers should ask as they conduct ongoing developmental research.

- What are the precise costs for the fixed assets the entrepreneur needs to purchase (backed up by references to industrial equipment and similar catalogues)?

- What are the precise costs for the needed insurance (backed up by a quotation from an insurance broker)?

- What are the correct wage and salary costs for the human resources the entrepreneur needs to hire (backed up by data indicating the wage and salary amounts for comparable positions in the region in which the company will operate)?

- What are the assumptions and methods used to project revenues (backed up by evidence that the assumptions and methods are realistic)?

- What are the precise costs for the inventories the entrepreneur needs to purchase before they can start their business (backed up by evidence from wholesale catalogues and quotations from targeted suppliers)?

Methods

As with proof of concept and foundational research methods, both primary and secondary research should be employed for ongoing developmental research. To conduct the primary research, entrepreneurs should ask trusted and experienced people familiar with the industry and market for their answers to questions related to costs and other needed information. A part of this activity involves getting quotations from professionals like commercial real estate agents and commercial insurance agents. A mistake that some business plan writers make is to avoid talking with these professionals and instead believe that they can acquire all the good advice and actual costs they need from secondary research.

Secondary research for ongoing developmental research includes looking up costs and other needed information from online sources, like product catalogues. Entrepreneurs should be sure to look up relevant costs for industrial and commercial quality products. For example, office furniture purchased from a regular consumer retail outlet is likely not of the quality required for commercial and industrial workspaces.

Analysis Tools

© Jakub Zak/Shutterstock.com

There are various analysis tools designed to help researchers conduct research. The tools are designed for different purposes, and it is essential when conducting different types of analyses to apply the right tool for the type of analysis. It is also essential to conduct analyses at different levels (see Figure 8) so that a vital type of inquiry is not overlooked.

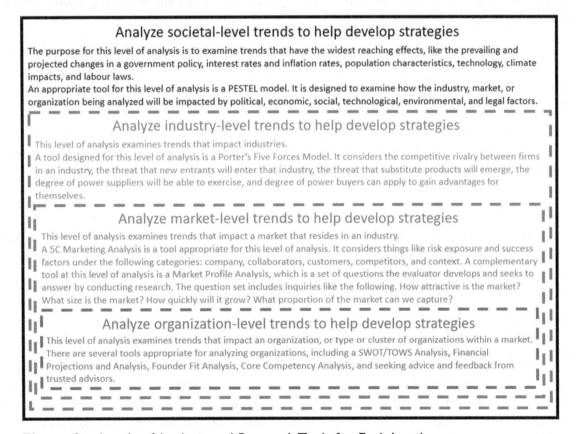

Analyze societal-level trends to help develop strategies

The purpose for this level of analysis is to examine trends that have the widest reaching effects, like the prevailing and projected changes in a government policy, interest rates and inflation rates, population characteristics, technology, climate impacts, and labour laws.
An appropriate tool for this level of analysis is a PESTEL model. It is designed to examine how the industry, market, or organization being analyzed will be impacted by political, economic, social, technological, environmental, and legal factors.

Analyze industry-level trends to help develop strategies

This level of analysis examines trends that impact industries.
A tool designed for this level of analysis is a Porter's Five Forces Model. It considers the competitive rivalry between firms in an industry, the threat that new entrants will enter that industry, the threat that substitute products will emerge, the degree of power suppliers will be able to exercise, and degree of power buyers can apply to gain advantages for themselves.

Analyze market-level trends to help develop strategies

This level of analysis examines trends that impact a market that resides in an industry.
A 5C Marketing Analysis is a tool appropriate for this level of analysis. It considers things like risk exposure and success factors under the following categories: company, collaborators, customers, competitors, and context. A complementary tool at this level of analysis is a Market Profile Analysis, which is a set of questions the evaluator develops and seeks to answer by conducting research. The question set includes inquiries like the following. How attractive is the market? What size is the market? How quickly will it grow? What proportion of the market can we capture?

Analyze organization-level trends to help develop strategies

This level of analysis examines trends that impact an organization, or type or cluster of organizations within a market. There are several tools appropriate for analyzing organizations, including a SWOT/TOWS Analysis, Financial Projections and Analysis, Founder Fit Analysis, Core Competency Analysis, and seeking advice and feedback from trusted advisors.

Figure 8.   Levels of Analysis and Research Tools for Each Level

(Illustration by Lee A. Swanson)

Whether evaluating entrepreneurial opportunities (sometimes called idea screening), assessing the operating environment to test the viability of an idea, adding necessary research information to a business plan, or conducting regular and routine scans of the operating environment, the analysis tools described in this section will be of use. Additionally, when a business plan writer or other researchers use the tools properly, they will end up with a more complete and useful analysis.

A mistake that many people make is to *start* their work by applying an analysis tool instead of first developing the questions for which they require answers. If someone conducting research mistakenly *starts* their analysis work by using a tool like a SWOT/TOWS Matrix framework (S = strengths, W = weaknesses, O = opportunities, and T = threats) or a Porter's Five Forces Model, they might generate some useful information, but this approach will likely frustrate them and make them feel like they have invested much time gathering information that, in the end, they cannot use.

It is almost always better for entrepreneurs to start the analysis work by developing sets of key questions for which they need answers (for examples, see the "Conducting the Three Types of Business Plan Research" section of this chapter). After compiling the sets of critical questions, the entrepreneur should seek targeted answers for them by applying the tools designed for each of the four levels of analysis, as shown in Figure 8.

By starting with sets of key questions when conducting research, entrepreneurs can achieve various research goals, like assessing new venture ideas, determining whether there is a viable market opportunity for a proposed venture, and analyzing and monitoring the operating environments in which existing businesses operate.

When conducting research, determine what outcomes should make their way into the business plan, and in what form they should appear. Include appropriately cited research results that are relevant and add value to the plan. The results included should support business plan objectives, like backing up strategies included in the promotion, pricing, and other parts of the plan.

One useful starting point when conducting research is to look up the North American Industry Classification System (NAICS) code relevant to the business type the entrepreneur is starting. The entrepreneur can then use that code to find a wealth of information about businesses in that category.

Societal-Level Analysis Tools

At a *societal level,* it is essential to understand each of the political, economic, social, technological, environmental, and legal (PESTEL) factors—and, more specifically, the trends affecting those factors—that will affect a proposed or existing venture. When including this research in a business plan, avoid using technical jargon and informal language that might distract readers.

Use an appropriate tool for societal-level analysis, like the PESTEL Model, to assess both the current situation and the likely changes that may affect a venture in the future. A PESTEL analysis includes the following components:

- Political factors affecting businesses include current and pending national, provincial or state, and municipal government policy. They also include the current and likely future philosophical foundations upon which political leaders make their decisions, pending or likely changes in the political environment, and political plans for taxes, infrastructure development, and many other things.

- Economic factors that might affect a venture include current and projected GDP growth for the region in which the business will operate (and maybe the regions in which the targeted customers will be), along with projected interest, inflation, and exchange rates.

- Social factors affecting businesses include population characteristics like age distribution and education levels. Projected changes in social conditions might also impact things like the projected demand patterns for products and services.
- Technological factors that impact organizations include new production processes, new products, and improved or deteriorating infrastructure.
- Environmental factors affecting businesses include the projected effects of climate change, regular weather occurrences, water availability, and smog and pollution issues.
- Legal factors that impact businesses include changes to labor laws, minimum wage rates, and liability issues.

Analyze the impact the trends might have on the venture. Among the potential impacts uncovered by useful analyses are projected cost increases, construction delays, increased legal costs, and the potential to include the newest computer or manufacturing technologies to gain a competitive advantage. Use the results from the analyses to develop strategies to include in the business plan. Consider how the business can take advantage of the opportunities uncovered by the trend analyses and how it can mitigate the risks identified by the analyses.

Industry-Level Analysis Tools

Analysis at the *industry level* should focus on the sector of the economy in which the business will operate. Apply Porter's (1985) Five Forces Model, or a similar tool, to evaluate industry-level factors. Avoid technical jargon, like *rivalry between firms*, and use more straightforward wording, like *competition*.

Market-Level Analysis Tools

To conduct a *market-level* analysis, use a tool to generate information about the part of the industry in which the business will compete. One appropriate tool is a 5C Market Analysis, which assesses the following factors: company, collaborators, customers, competitors, and context.

A complementary tool is a Market Profile Analysis, which is a set of questions designed to uncover information needed to develop plans to improve the proposed venture's success. The following are examples of the types of questions included in a market profile analysis:

- How attractive is the market?
- In what way are competitors expected to respond when the business enters the market?
- What is the current size of the market and how large is it expected to become?
- What are the current and projected growth rates?
- At what stage of the development cycle is the market?
- What level of profits can be expected in the market?
- What proportion of the market can be captured? What will be the cost to capture this proportion, and what is the cost to capture the proportion required for business sustainability?

Before a new business starts, the customers that the new business wishes to attract either already purchase the product or service from a competitor to the new business or do not yet purchase the product or service at all.

A new venture's customers, therefore, must come from one of two sources. They must be attracted away from existing competitors or be convinced to make different choices about where they spend their money, so they purchase the new venture's product or service instead of spending their money in other ways. This means an entrepreneur must decide from where they will attract their customers, and how they will do so. They must understand the competitive environment.

According to Porter (1996), strategy is about doing different things than competitors or doing similar things but in different ways. In order to develop an effective strategy, an entrepreneur must understand the competition.

To understanding the competitive environment, entrepreneurs must do the following:

- Determine who the current direct and indirect competitors are and who the future competitors might be.

- Understand the similarities and differences in quality, price, competitive advantages, and other factors that exist between the proposed business and the existing competitors.

- Establish whether the proposed business can offer different products or services—or the same products or services in different ways—to attract enough customers to meet the sales goals.

- Anticipate how the competitors will react in response to the new venture's entry into the market.

Organization-Level Analysis Tools

At the *organization level*, both the internal organizational trends and the external market profile trends should be analyzed. There are several tools for conducting an internal organizational analysis, and an entrepreneur should apply several of them because they serve different purposes.

Tools like a SWOT/TOWS Analysis can help an entrepreneur formulate and evaluate potential strategies to leverage organizational strengths, overcome or minimize weaknesses, take advantage of opportunities, and overcome or minimize threats. An entrepreneur must also conduct *financial analyses* and consider the *founder fit* and the *competencies* a venture should possess.

When conducting a SWOT/TOWS Analysis, an entrepreneur has more work to do after developing the list of internal strengths and weaknesses and external opportunities and threats. They must then develop strategies to take advantage of the identified strengths and opportunities while mitigating the weaknesses and threats. To do this, they need to consider those elements in pairs. For example, they can start by going through the list of identified threats one by one while considering how to develop strategies to mitigate each of them by using the identified strengths. They should then go through the same exercise by going through the list of opportunities to see how they can leverage their strengths through strategies to take advantage of the opportunities. In other words, a SWOT/TOWS Analysis can develop strategies that do the following:

- Leverage strengths to take advantage of opportunities
- Leverage strengths to overcome threats
- Mitigate weaknesses by taking advantage of opportunities
- Mitigate weaknesses while minimizing the potential threats or the potential outcomes from threats

To analyze the resources available to support a business's strategy, apply a *VRIO Framework* analysis (Barney, 1997; Barney & Hesterly, 2006). While conceptualizing the resource-based view (RBV), Barney (1997) identified the following four considerations regarding resources and their ability to help a firm gain a competitive advantage. Together, the following four questions make up the VRIO Framework, which can assess a firm's capacity and determine what competencies a venture should have. To use this tool, determine whether competencies are valuable, rare, inimitable, and organized in a way that they can be exploited.

- Value—Is a particular resource (financial, physical, technological, organizational, human, reputational, innovative) valuable to a firm because it helps it take advantage of opportunities or eliminate threats?
- Rarity—Is a particular resource rare in that it is controlled by or available to relatively few others?
- Imitability—Is a particular resource difficult to imitate so that those who have it can retain cost advantages over those who might try to obtain or duplicate it?
- Organization—Are the resources available to a firm useful to it because it is organized and ready to exploit them?

To assess the financial attractiveness of the venture, analyze the following:

- Similar firms in the industry
  - Entrepreneurs should conduct ratio and financial analysis to help determine inventory turnover, working capital, operating efficiency, and other measures of firm success as compared to other companies in the industry.
- Projected market share
  - By analysing the key industry players' relative market share, an entrepreneur can make judgments about how their proposed venture might fare within the industry.
  - Information from the market profile and key industry player analyses can be used to help project a proposed firm's market share.
- Margin analysis
  - By projecting a proposed business's margins, an entrepreneur can assess how they differ from those of similar firms.
  - Useful information about margins might come from financial analysis, market profile analysis, and other sources found using NAICS codes searches.
- Break-even analysis
  - An entrepreneur should calculate and evaluate a proposed firm's break-even sales volume and the break-even in sales dollars.
  - A key question is how long it will take and how many resources will be required to generate sufficient volume to sustain the venture.
- Pro forma analysis
  - An entrepreneur must analyze the projected financial statements for their proposed business to assess its viability.

- Sensitivity analysis
  - Sensitivity analysis involves changing the values for some key variables in the financial model to assess the impact if important assumptions do not come true.
- Return on investment (ROI) projections
  - Entrepreneurs should project their ROI from undertaking the venture, and that of their targeted investors from potentially investing in it.
  - It is also important for entrepreneurs to assess their opportunity cost of investing time and money in the business.

Founder fit is an important consideration for entrepreneurs screening venture opportunities. While there are plenty of examples of entrepreneurs successfully starting all types of businesses, "technical capability can be an important if not all-important factor in pursuing venture success" (Vesper, 1996, p. 149). Factors such as the experience, training, credentials, reputation, and social capital an entrepreneur has can play an essential role in their success or failure in starting a new venture. Even when an entrepreneur can recruit expert help through business partners or employees, it might be vital that he or she also possesses the technical skills required in that particular kind of business.

A common and useful way to help screen venture options is to seek input from experts, peers, mentors, business associates, and perhaps other stakeholders like potential customers and direct family members.

Presenting the Research Results in the Business Plan

Rather than showing an analysis tool used, like a Porter's Five Forces model, in the body of the business plan, the entrepreneur should show the *results of the analysis* in the places throughout the plan where they are used to support strategies and present important information. If a business plan writer believes it will add value to the plan to inform potential readers about the research analysis tools they used, they can describe their analysis in an appendix. All appendices should be referenced in the body of the plan.

Chapter Summary

By applying the right tools to analyze the operating environment at each of the societal, industry, market, and organization levels, entrepreneurs screen venture ideas, plan new venture development, and potentially detect factors that might affect their business operations.

Exercises

Exercise 2.1—NAICS Code

Look up the relevant NAICS code for a business type of interest and explore the information that can be found using that code.

Exercise 2.2—Research Analyses Worksheets

Use the Research Analyses Worksheets (Appendix A) to plan and organize the research when building the business plan.

Cross-Chapter Case—Tech World Pro Part 2

Research to Screen Ideas

Talia and Malik Garcia have decided to start a retail business that they can run from their current home city, because they do not want to move. To help them decide what kind of business to start, they took their last vacation to a large city known for its trendy ventures, read entrepreneurship and trend books and magazines, spoke to business brokers about the kinds of businesses for sale in their community, and considered their personal interests in outdoor activities, children's clothing and toys, music, and electronics. They saw some interesting businesses on their trip, and read about others. They did not find any businesses for sale that interested them except for a couple, but they were concerned about why they were for sale and were suspicious that there was not enough consumer demand in their city to support them. In the end, they narrowed their choices down to a sporting goods store, a music store, and a computer retail outlet that also provides service work for computer owners.

Talia and Malik have decided to use the Research Analyses Worksheets and follow the a key-questions-first approach to conduct proof of concept research. Their first goal was to determine which, if any, of the three options might lead to a successful business in their city. Second, if more than one of the potential businesses appear to be viable, they want to use their research to choose the best option. So far, they have developed the following key questions for which they intend to get answers to help them determine the viability of the sporting goods store idea.

Worksheet 1—Key Questions

Proof of Concept Research: Can the business concept be converted into a viable and sustainable business entity?	
Key Questions	Levels of Analysis and Tools
• What are the relevant societal trends impacting sports and leisure?	Societal-level trends • PESTEL analysis
• How many sporting goods stores can a population of the local size support? • How many sporting goods stores are there in the local market? • How saturated is the local sporting goods market? • Are there plans for new stores of this kind to open in the local market? • Which, if any, of the current stores are planning to expand? Why? • Which, if any, of the current stores are planning to scale down or close? • What are the current sporting and leisure trends affecting sales in the sporting good market, and how are sales being affected?	Market-level trends • Market profile analysis

Cross-Chapter Case Activities—Part 2

1. Complete the key questions worksheet Talia and Malik started for the sporting goods store option.

2. Complete key questions worksheets for the music and computer store ideas.

3. Look up the NAICS codes for the three business types and review the types of information available, like industry average financial ratios, that can be found using the codes.

© dotshock/Shutterstock.com

Chapter 3

Using a Business Model to Start the Business Plan

Learning Objectives

After completing this chapter, you will be able to:

◆ Describe what a business model is

◆ Analyze existing and proposed businesses to determine what business models they are applying and what business models they plan to apply (chapter exercise)

◆ Develop and analyze alternative business models for new entrepreneurial ventures

◆ Use a business model as a start point for developing a business plan

Overview

This chapter introduces the business model concept. A common way to depict a business model is through the Business Model Canvas, a framework that categorizes nine elements of a business model. The chapter also outlines general guidelines for using a business model as a start for developing a business plan (Figure 9).

© Photon photo/Shutterstock.com

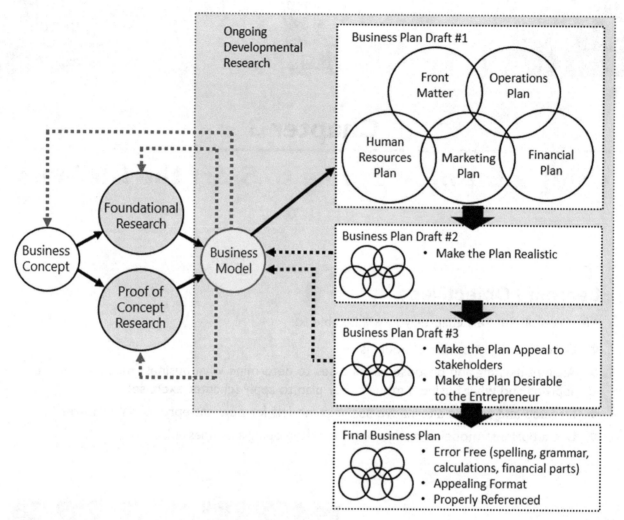

Figure 9. Business Model

(Illustration by Lee A. Swanson)

What Are Business Models?

Magretta (2002) described business models as "stories that explain how enterprises work" (p. 87) and Osterwalder, Pigneur, and Clark (2010) noted that they reveal "the rationale of how an organization creates, delivers, and captures value" (p. 14). Chatterjee (2013) said that "A business is about selling what you make for a profit. A business model is a configuration (activity systems) of what the business does (activities) and what it invests in (resources) based on the logic that drives the profits for a specific business" (p. 97).

Osterwalder et al. (2010) said that a start up is something entirely different than an ongoing venture. A start up should not be viewed as a smaller version of a company because it requires very different skills to start up a company than it does to operate one. A start up that is still a start up after some time has passed—maybe after a couple of years for some kinds of start ups—is a failed enterprise since it has not converted into an ongoing venture. Entrepreneurs who develop a business model for their ventures that deliver value to the targeted customers and the entrepreneur stand a better chance of converting their start up into an ongoing venture.

© Dustit/Shutterstock.com

The Business Model Canvas

The business model canvas (Osterwalder et al., 2010) is made up of nine parts that, together, describe the business model (see Figure 10). This model can be used by entrepreneurs using the lean start up approach (Ries, 2011). For more information on the lean start up, see Chapter 1. Entrepreneurs can also use it to conceptualize their business before writing a business plan.

According to Osterwalder et al. (2010), the things we typically teach people in business school are geared to helping people survive in more substantial, ongoing businesses. What is taught—including organizational structures, reporting lines, managing sales teams, advertising, and similar topics—is not designed to help students understand how a start up works and how to deal with the volatile nature of new ventures. The Business Model Canvas tool is meant to help us understand start ups better.

The Business Model Canvas tool is intended to be applied when business operations can be started on a small scale, and adjustments can be made continually until the evolving business model works in real life. This contrasts with the more traditional approach of preplanning everything, going through the set up and start up processes, and ending up with a business venture that opens for business one day without having proven at all that the business model it is founded upon will even work (Osterwalder et al., 2010). These traditional start ups sometimes flounder along as the owners find that their plans are not quite working out and they try to make adjustments on the fly. It can be challenging to adjust, though, because the processes are already set up. For example, sales teams might be in the field trying to make sales and blaming the product developers for the difficulty they are having, and the product developers might be blaming the sales teams for not being able to sell the product correctly. The real issue might be that the company is not meeting customers' needs, and they do not have a suitable mechanism for detecting, understanding, and fixing this problem.

Whether applying the lean start up approach (Ries, 2011) or planning to write a business plan for a new venture, an entrepreneur needs a business model. Please refer to Figure 10 and the sections following it to learn how to use the Business Model Canvas (Osterwalder et al., 2010) to develop the foundation needed for a business plan.

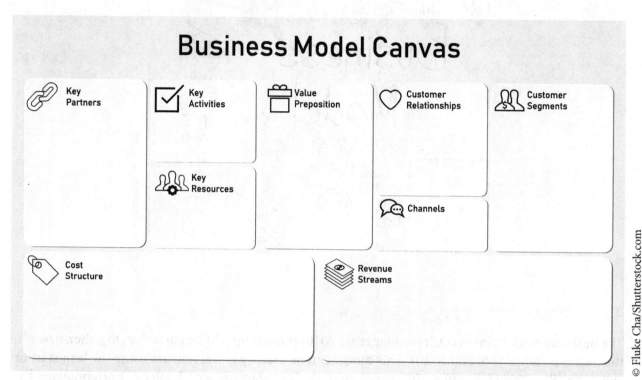

Figure 10. Business Model Canvas

The following elements of the Business Model Canvas were taken, with permission, from http://www.businessmodelgeneration.com.

- Key partners
  - Who are our key partners?
  - Who are our key suppliers?
  - Which key resources are we acquiring from partners?
  - Which key activities do partners perform?
  - Motivations for partnerships: optimization and economy, reduction of risk and uncertainty, acquisition of particular resources and activities
- Key activities
  - What key activities do our value propositions require?
  - Our distribution channels?
  - Customer relationships?
  - Revenue streams?
  - Categories: production, problem–solving, platform/network

- Key resources
  - What key resources do our value propositions require?
  - Our distribution channels?
  - Customer relationships?
  - Revenue streams?
  - Types of resources: physical; intellectual (brand patents, copyrights, data); human; financial
- Value propositions
  - What value do we deliver to the customer?
  - Which one of our customer's problems are we helping to solve?
  - What bundles of products and services are we offering to each customer segment?
  - Which customer needs are we satisfying?
  - Characteristics: newness, performance, customization, "getting the job done," design, brand and status, price, cost reduction, risk reduction, accessibility, convenience/usability
- Customer relationships
  - What type of relationship does each of our customer segments expect us to establish and maintain with them?
  - Which ones have we established?
  - How are they integrated with the rest of our business model?
  - How costly are they?
  - Examples: personal assistance, dedicated personal assistance, self–service, automated services, communities, cocreation
- Customer segments
  - For whom are we creating value?
  - Who are our most important customers?
  - Mass market, niche market, segmented, diversified, multisided platform
- Channels
  - Through which channels do our customer segments want to be reached?
  - How are we reaching them now?
  - How are our channels integrated?
  - Which ones work best?
  - Which ones are most cost-efficient?
  - How are we integrating them with customer routines?
  - Channel phases
    - Awareness—How do we raise awareness about our company's products and services?
    - Evaluation—How do we help customers evaluate our organization's value proposition?
    - Purchase—How do we allow customers to purchase specific products and services?
    - Delivery—How do we deliver a value proposition to customers?
    - After-sales—How do we provide postpurchase customer support?

- Revenue streams
  - For what value are our customers willing to pay?
  - For what do they currently pay?
  - How are they currently paying?
  - How would they prefer to pay?
  - How much does each revenue stream contribute to overall revenues?
  - Types: asset sale, usage fee, subscription fees, lending/renting/leasing, licensing, brokerage fees, advertising
  - Fixed pricing: list price, product feature dependent, customer segment dependent, volume dependent
  - Dynamic pricing: negotiation (bargaining), yield management, real-time market
- Cost structure
  - What are the most important costs inherent in our business model?
  - Which key resources are the most expensive?
  - Which key activities are the most expensive?
  - Is our business more cost driven (leanest cost structure, low price value proposition, maximum automation, extensive outsourcing) or value driven (focused on value creation, premium value proposition)?
  - Sample characteristics: fixed costs (salaries, rents, utilities), variable costs, economies of scale, economies of scope

Entrepreneurs should add assumptions and descriptions to the nine components to create an initial business model. They should then replace those initial assumptions and descriptions with newer and better information as they conduct research and learn new things as the business model evolves. Osterwalder et al. (2010) suggest that the entrepreneur directly interacts with potential customers as the business model develops. The owner will then better understand what the market wants and how the business should operate. After the entrepreneur gains that knowledge, salespeople and other employees might begin working with customers. By working directly with customers and making adjustments to operations as needed to satisfy those customers, an entrepreneur is conducting a form of market research.

Detailed Guidelines for Developing Business Plan Drafts

Review Section "General Guidelines for Developing Business Plans" in Chapter 1. The following provides more detailed directions for using business models as a start point for developing business plans.

- Business plan writers should develop a comprehensive business model as a start point for developing a draft business plan. The elements of a business model must be reflected throughout the draft business plan in the appropriate sections as there is no single section in which a business model can be presented.

- Writers should avoid repetition in a business plan. They should usually only state something one time in a business plan, provided they place the information in the part of the plan where it fits the best. Only in rare cases might it be necessary to state something a second time. Rather than restate information in a business plan, writers should cross-reference their work by referring readers to other sections of the business plan where they can get relevant information.

- It is often easiest for business plan writers first to include **what** they know and **what** they plan to do in the first draft of a business plan. After doing that, they should revisit each section and add the details that thoroughly answer the **why, who, when, where**, and **how** questions.

- Whenever writers include graphs, charts, and appendices, they must reference them in the central part of the business plan.

- Business plan writers must use decisive language in their written work. They should avoid using phrases that weaken the plan. An example of such a phrase is one that leaves a reader with the impression that the writer is unsure about something or that they have drawn a conclusion without adequate evidence to back it up.

Writing the Draft Business Plan

Although there are various ways to approach the task of writing a draft business plan, the following describes one practical approach:

- Business plan writers should use the Research Analyses Worksheets available in Appendix A to guide their research activities throughout the business planning process.

- They should use the Word and Excel templates accessible through Appendices B and C to develop their plan. An effective way to avoid losing work is to frequently save the Word and Excel files using new names based on a reverse date protocol. For example, after adding important information to the Excel template, the writer should save it under a file name starting with the date written numerically in this style: yyyymmdd. If the current date is February 19, 2024, the file name should look something like this: **20240219 ABC Company Draft Business Plan**.

- The writer should then add the elements of the business model into the Word and Excel business plan templates. As there is no single section in the business plan Word template in which to describe a business model, so the writer should incorporate its elements into the appropriate sections of the business plan.

- The business plan writer should fill in the sections of the business plan templates while flagging, perhaps by using a different color font, any information based on assumptions or weak references. When replacing the assumptions with real information backed up by valid references, they should change the font to the standard color. For example, a business plan writer might include estimated costs for office equipment and furniture and flag the explanations and numbers in red text to indicate they were assumptions. The writer might then consult an online supplier catalogue after which they replace the explanations and cost figures with the descriptions and numbers from the catalogue, add an in-text citation and reference list entry for the catalogue site, and change the font color from red to black to indicate that the entry is no longer based on an assumption.

Chapter Summary

This chapter described business models and presented the Business Model Canvas as a tool that entrepreneurs can use to develop and define their business models. It also outlines general guidelines for developing a business plan starting from a business model.

Exercises

Exercise 3.1—Business Model Canvas

Use the Business Model Canvas to develop a business model for a new or existing business.

Exercise 3.2—Analyze a Business Plan to Determine the Business Model

Analyze a business plan for a proposed business to determine its business model elements.

Cross-Chapter Case—Tech World Pro Part 3

The Initial Business Model

Talia and Malik Garcia used the Research Analyses Worksheets to help them follow a key-questions-first approach to conduct proof of concept research for a sporting goods store, music store, and computer store that also provides service work for computer owners. They found that the local market was too saturated to support another sporting goods store and they were concerned about the small margins and future outlook for a music store, although they considered it to be a viable option with a good founder fit (meaning they felt they had the right knowledge and skill sets to make that type of business a success). However, they felt the best option for them was the computer store.

The Garcias settled on Tech World Pro as a tentative name for their business, pending confirmation that the name was available and not registered by another individual or company. They learned that they should have a lawyer conduct a name search to see whether they could use it. If so, they should have the lawyer register the name Tech World Pro with the proper authorities to protect it for their use only. They also determined that for tax and liability reasons, after registering the name, they should incorporate the business instead of operating it as a partnership.

While considering their personal goals and means, and taking into account what they learned while conducting their research, Talia and Malik tentatively planned to open their new store to the public on March 1, 2024. They also found a building in a part of the city they liked that they could purchase and take possession of in January, 2024 to allow them to renovate the space and fully set up the store before making their first sale on March 1. However, they realized that before finalizing those plans, they had lots of work to do.

The first thing they knew they had to do was develop an initial business model before they could start their business planning. They used the business model canvas to decide upon an initial structure for their business. The following summarizes the couple's business model deliberations:

- Value Propositions
  - Pending further research to ensure that targeted customers would, in fact, view it as of enough value to them to warrant them spending their money at the business, Talia and Malik believed they could sell computer systems, components, and supplies, and provide hardware and software set up, installation, and repair services for computer owners in their defined geographic region because it was underserved by businesses that provided those products and services.
  - They also felt they could provide products, customer service, and services that their targeted customers would trust and value more than they would from any of the existing competitors operating in the region.

- Customer Segments
  - Talia and Malik planned to initially focus on consumer sales versus commercial and industrial customers. This was, in part, because Talia's parents ran a restaurant and her aunt owned a clothing store chain, and the couple could draw on the extensive family experience in consumer sales.
  - They felt that they needed to consider the aspects of geographic, psychographic, behavioral, and possibly even demographic segmentation.
    - Geographically, Talia and Malik felt that they should focus on attracting customers residing in the eastern half of their city (as delineated by a main highway dividing the city's eastern and western sides) because their main competitor was well established on the western side. However, they also believed that they could develop product and service strategies to attract customers from anywhere in the city and within a trading area defined as the region extending out 100 km (62 miles) from the city center.
    - Psychographically, they believed they could target people who were interested in computers and electronics and who preferred to purchase brand name instead of generic products.
    - Behaviorally, the couple felt that they should target consumers who tended to be loyal to brands and companies they liked versus those who preferred to shop around for the lowest price product and who sought convenience when purchasing service work from companies.
    - Demographically, they wondered whether they should target people and families in higher income brackets. They did not feel that age, gender, education levels, occupations, ethnicity, and other demographic factors were relevant when determining who they should target as customers.

- Customer Relationships
  - As indicated by their value proposition deliberations, Talia and Malik planned to develop and maintain customer relationships that would help their company attract customers away from the competitors.
- Key Partners
  - Considering their tentative customer segment choices, Talia and Malik felt that they should strive to build and maintain key partnerships with selected computer wholesalers with established and well-known brand names.
  - Based on advice from their current mentors (Talia's parents and aunt), the couple believed that they should purposefully work to establish and maintain partnership relationships with other suppliers, delivery companies (rather than deliver products themselves to customers, when asked), and with any potential customers or contacts—like acquaintances who worked with organizations that, on a regular basis, purchased several (or a lot) of computers, computer components, or software packages. They also felt that they might be able to position Tech World Pro as a preferred supplier of computer hardware or software support for those types of organizations if they could establish the right relationships with them. However, they viewed this as a longer term strategy as they planned to initially target the consumer, rather than the commercial and industrial markets.
- Key Activities
  - The Garcias knew they had to rely on Talia's parents and aunt to understand the full range of key activities required to set up, start up, and establish the processes required to operate a consumer retail business like Tech World Pro. To help them get a start on their business plan, after talking about business processes with their mentors, the couple sketched several process flowcharts showing how they thought they would handle things such as hiring employees, managing them, scheduling the workers (including themselves as they planned to actively work in the business), securely handling money generated from sales, and generally running the business.
- Key Resources
  - Talia and Malik viewed the expertise offered by their current mentors, Talia's parents and aunt, as key resources, although they felt they would benefit by finding additional mentors who could help them enter the computer sales and service market. When thinking about their longer term plans, they decided they could use some advisors with experience in commercial and industrial sales.
  - In terms of financial resources, they had their $78,000 in savings along with valid and ready commitments of financial support from both sets of parents and Talia's aunt.
  - Considering time as a needed resource, Talia had decided that she was prepared to resign from her position with the bank so she could work on the business while looking after 3-year-old Owen, with some help from her parents, who now spent minimal time operating their well-established restaurant because they had an experienced and capable team in place. Malik would continue working as a teacher for the remaining four months of the current school year, and the first four months of the next year after which he planned to quit to work full time on the business with Talia.

- o The company would need physical assets, including a building. Talia and Malik planned to accept Talia's aunt's offer to help them financially by providing them with a down payment on a mortgage loan to purchase land and a building.
- o Regarding human resources, the couple planned to actively work in the business and hire all other needed workers.
- Channels
  - o The couple expected that most of their sales would occur in-person in-store, including their hardware and software installation, repair, and maintenance service work.
- Cost Structure
  - o Talia and Malik expected that their main costs would be to pay their workers and cover the principal and loan interest costs on their building mortgage. They also expected to have substantial merchandise purchase costs.
- Revenue Streams
  - o Talia and Malik planned to sell three product lines:
    - Computer systems (including laptop computers and full desktop systems)
    - Computer components (including mouses, keypads, monitors, printers, scanners, external file storage devices, and other items)
    - Computer supplies (such as printer paper, keyboard cleaning supplies, and many other items like this)
  - o They also planned to hire computer hardware and software technicians to set up, install, and repair customers' machines and programs for a fee.

Cross-Chapter Case Activities—Part 3

1. Starting with a new Business Plan Word Template (see Appendix B), enter the business name in the appropriate places and begin to develop the written business plan by doing the following:
   - In the Value Proposition part of the Front Matter section, begin writing the value proposition based on the information Talia and Malik included in the initial business model.
   - In the appropriate Operations Plan sections, indicate that the business will be a corporation and write some rationale for choosing that type of legal form. Enter the preliminary information about business processes and other items indicated in the initial business model.
   - In the Human Resources Plan and Marketing Plan sections, record the relevant information from the initial business model about hiring plans, market segmentation and target markets, product strategies, and so on.
   - In the Financial Plan section (or possibly the Operations Plan, if the information seems to be better placed there), note the plan to conduct a business name search, register the chosen business name, and record estimates for the legal costs those for activities, and for incorporating the business. Add any other information relevant to the company's financial model.

2. Save the Word document using the *best practice* of applying a reverse date protocol when naming the file. For example, you should name your file something like the following (assuming that you start developing your financial model on June 30, 2021): *20210630 Tech World Pro Draft Business Plan.docx.*

3. Starting with a new Business Plan Excel Template (see Appendix C):

   • In the blue input cells on the ControlPanel Worksheet, enter the business name, *Tech World Pro*, and the financial sheet start date of *January 1, 2024.*

Save the Excel file using the reverse date file naming protocol. For example, you use name something like the following for your Excel file: *20210630 Tech World Pro Draft Business Plan.xlsx.*

© dotshock/Shutterstock.com

Chapter 4

First Business Plan Draft: Front Matter

Learning Objectives

After completing this chapter, you will be able to:

◆ Describe the elements of the front matter part of a business plan

◆ Develop the front matter for a comprehensive business plan draft

Overview

This chapter describes an approach to writing the first draft of the front matter part of a comprehensive business plan (Figure 11). It describes the elements of a business plan located before the operations, human resources, marketing, and financial plan sections. Those elements include the executive summary—which is the last part of the business plan that a writer should finish—along with the introduction part.

Business plan writers often describe **what** they know and **what** they are planning in the first draft of a business plan. To strengthen their work, they should describe **why** they have those plans, **who** will carry them out and otherwise be involved in implementing the plans, **when** the plans will be carried out, **where** everything will happen, and **how** their plans will materialize.

Weak business plans emphasize descriptions of **what** the entrepreneur knows and **what** they plan to do. In contrast, robust plans complement those descriptions of **why**, **who**, **when**, **where**, and **how** to back up and explain the plans about *what* the entrepreneur is planning to do.

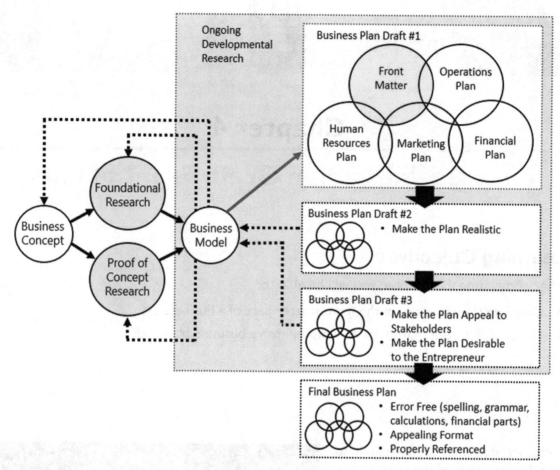

Figure 11.   Front Matter

(Illustration by Lee A. Swanson)

Front Matter Contents

The front matter part of a business plan starts with a suitable title page followed by an executive summary to provide readers with an overview of the overall plan. The front matter also includes some essential structural components, like a detailed table of contents along with lists of the tables and figures contained in the business plan.

The Introduction part of the business plan is also part of the front matter. It includes crucial contextual information in the Business Description section and, in the Business Need part, an assessment of how research results indicate that enough targeted customers will be willing to purchase enough of the business's products and services to make the venture financially sustainable. The Value Proposition section describes the benefits the business will deliver to its customers. A Vision indicates what the entrepreneur aspires for the business to become. The Mission describes what the business will do, the Values Statements indicate the foundation upon which the business will operate, and the Major Goals provide targeted readers with information about the business's anticipated accomplishments that might appeal to them.

The key questions addressed by the Introduction section include the following:

- What will this business do?
- Is there a market need for this business?

- What value will the business generate for its targeted customers?
- What does the entrepreneur aspire for this business to become?
- Why will the business existence over the next while?
- Upon what value-based foundation will the entrepreneur build the business?
- What significant goals will this business achieve that will be meaningful for the targeted business plan readers, including potential investors?

Title Page

To make it more appealing for targeted readers, business plan writers should include catchy, professional, and appropriate graphics on the title page.

Executive Summary

The Executive Summary is the last thing a business plan writer should write because it provides a summary of the vital information contained in the plan. For information on the Executive Summary section, see Chapter 12.

© fizkes/Shutterstock.com

Table of Contents

All business plans follow a relatively standard format that meets the needs of targeted readers. Review the Table of Contents on the Word template accessible through Appendix B. The Table of Contents in the Word template can be automatically generated using the word processing software features.

List of Tables

The List of Tables in the Word template can be automatically generated using the features built into the template.

When including a table, figure, appendix, or other feature in a business plan, the writer must reference the item within the plan's text.

List of Figures

Use the features in the Word template to automatically generate the List of Figures.

Introduction

Write between one and five brief introductory paragraphs to introduce the reader to what is in this section of the plan. If relevant, briefly describe the purpose of the plan.

The Introduction should *tell the story* of the business concept while providing evidence—through well-referenced primary and secondary research results—to show that the business fulfills a market need and that targeted customers will be willing to purchase the product or service from the business.

© KoOlyphoto/Shutterstock.com

It is sometimes appropriate to indicate in the Introduction section what the purpose of the plan is.

Write this section to appeal to targeted readers.

Business Description

Describe the business concept in about three or four paragraphs. If relevant, explain the history behind the business idea, including how the concept evolved. Entrepreneurs can use this section to describe why they wanted to start this kind of business, why they named it as they did, and other relevant contextual information to help readers understand the background behind the business idea.

It might also add value for targeted readers for the business plan writer to include a description in this section of the history behind the idea and the evolution of the business concept.

Business Need

Use this section to describe in about three to five paragraphs why the business is needed. The goal is to *prove to readers that the market needs the business or will at least support it enough for it to be a viable venture.*

The paragraphs in this section should include several *relevant references* that support the idea that this business should exist as described in the business plan. Back up all claims of fact with solid research (see Chapter 2 and use the Research Analysis Worksheets in Appendix A).

Value Proposition

Describe what the business's *value proposition* is. The value proposition outlines the benefits the venture promises to deliver *to its customers*. A value proposition indicates why the business provides something that targeted customers will be willing to pay enough to ensure that the venture can sustain itself financially. It explains how the business idea solves a problem for the targeted customers or otherwise does something for them such that they will want to purchase the product or service from the proposed business instead of from a competitor.

In some cases, business plan writers can include a secondary value proposition that explains why it should be appealing for investors to invest in the business.

Vision

A good vision concisely, using a few memorable words, outlines what the owner intends for the venture to be. It is what the owner aspires for his or her venture to become in the future. It is not a description of what the business does at start-up.

The best vision statements inspire stakeholders associated with the venture to achieve great things through it.

An entrepreneur needs to understand what it means to realize their vision before they can craft strategies to achieve it. So, they should decide what it will look like to realize their vision. For example, if an entrepreneur preparing a business plan for a retail store decides that their vision is to be the most recognized retailer in the region for that category of product, what does that mean? Will they have company-owned stores in the larger centers across the region? Will they instead implement a franchise business model and achieve the vision that way? Alternatively, will they sell the product across the region using e-commerce or a distributor system? Perhaps to them, being "the most recognized retailer in the region" mean that they will have a single store that will gain recognition by winning awards and having a high profile rather than by making lots of sales.

A vision should stand on its own without the need for further explanation. Do not include extra sentences to explain it. The detailed explanations should appear throughout the rest of the plan.

Many business plan writers write their vision and leave it at that. After articulating a good vision, entrepreneurs need to develop and implement strategies designed to achieve their vision, not just fulfill their current mission.

Mission

A mission statement indicates what a venture does and why it exists. It generally describes what the business will do at start-up or within a few months of that time when it hopes to operate in a somewhat routine fashion. A mission might briefly describe the business strategy and philosophy.

Mission statements should be very brief. They are often only a few sentences or a short paragraph in length.

Entrepreneurs can get a start on their mission statement by listing the product and service categories they expect to provide. They can then reframe that list into a simple and relatively short statement describing what their business will provide or do when it opens (or within a few months of opening).

Values

Values statements describe the fundamental values that will guide everything the business will do. They outline the personal commitments that members of the organization must make and what they should consider to be important. Values statements should define how individuals associated with the venture behave and interact with each other. They should help the business plan reader understand the type of culture and operating environment the owner intends to develop for the venture.

If there are only one or two values statements, this section will look incomplete and probably strange. A business plan writer should *list and briefly describe* a reasonable number of values—usually about five or six—that are inherently important to the entrepreneur.

To test the potential effectiveness of proposed values and values statements, say the words "we value" before verbalizing a proposed value. Then, consider whether the phrase accurately reflects the entrepreneur's deeply held beliefs that will influence business operations. Also, reflect on whether the phrase can help guide employee recruitment, training, and management activities. Consider whether the value statement can provide the entrepreneur with guidance when developing and implementing strategies and plans for the business. Well-crafted values statements should help targeted readers understand the type of culture and operating environment the entrepreneur wishes to develop for their business.

When writing the remainder of the business plan, incorporate the values, although not necessarily explicitly, into the plans recorded in the Introduction, Human Resources, Marketing, and Financial Plan sections. Strong values statements leave targeted readers with a strong feeling that the entrepreneur is committed to building the business on a solid foundation.

Major Goals

The Major Goals section is the second last section the business plan writer should finish, just before they finalize the Executive Summary. The goals should be designed to appeal to the targeted readers, and each goal should correspond to an essential and relevant accomplishment described in the business plan. For more information on writing the Major Goals section, see Chapter 12.

Chapter Summary

This chapter described the components of the Front Matter part of a business plan, including the Introduction section and its subsections.

Exercises

Exercise 4.1—Writing the Front Matter

Use the Business Plan Word Template (Appendix B) to begin writing the front matter part of the business plan (except for the Executive Summary and the Major Goals).

Cross-Chapter Case—Tech World Pro Part 4

The Initial Front Matter

Talia and Malik Garcia have developed their initial business model while understanding it to be an ever-changing structure as they continue to gather new and relevant data through research. Their initial business model included their perspectives on their proposed venture's value proposition for targeted customers. After receiving some advice from Talia's parents, who were experienced entrepreneurs, the couple decided to spend some time making decisions about where they wanted to go with their company and how they would get there.

The couple view their company vision as an aspirational end point they may be able to arrive at in the future, perhaps in 10 or 15 years time. It is like a beacon at which they should aim when developing strategy. They see their company mission as a statement describing what their business does upon start-up, or within the first few months of starting. Their values statements should provide them with the guidelines within which they will operate as they develop the company from its current state (or, in their case, its initial state)—as described by the mission—to its future desired state as indicated by the vision. The values statements should also indicate the desired company culture and provide guidance as to how to attain or maintain it.

Based on their understanding of visions, missions, and values statements, the Garcias see their company as offering all of the goods and services they outlined in their business model at, or shortly after business start up. As guiding values, they chose fairness, honesty, excellent leadership and management, and business and environmental sustainability. Although they hadn't yet crafted the brief, single-sentence descriptive statements for each of the values, they knew they wanted to reflect a desire to treat customers, staff, community, and suppliers and other partners fairly and honestly, in part by implementing well-conceived management and leadership strategies that had been objectively proven to work for small companies like theirs. As a reflection of their love of nature and the outdoors, Talia and Malik wanted to distinguish their company as one that embraced the most up-to-date waste reduction and recycling methods, and, where possible, operated in as energy efficient a manner as possible.

Cross-Chapter Case Activities—Part 4

1. Open the Business Plan Word Template on which you started to develop the written business plan. Go to the front matter section in which you started to articulate a value statement based on the Garcia's business model. Begin to fill in the business description, business need (backed up by references to any available research outcomes), and the vision, mission, and values sections based on the couple's deliberations in those areas.

2. Save the revised Word document by using a slightly new name to reflect the current date in the first part of the file name. For example, if you completed the revision on July 2, 2021, the revised file would be named *20210702 Tech World Pro Draft Business Plan.docx.*

© dotshock/Shutterstock.com

Chapter 5

First Business Plan Draft: Operations Plan

Learning Objectives

After completing this chapter, you will be able to:

◆ Develop the operations plan for a comprehensive business plan draft while ensuring that all parts of the business plan are fully integrated

Overview

This chapter describes the elements of the Operations Plan part of a comprehensive business plan (Figure 12). As with the front matter part of a business plan, when developing the Operations Plan, writers often first describe *what* they plan to do. They then add more detail and substance to the section by adding the necessary *why*, *who*, *when*, *where*, and *how* accounts to this part of the plan.

© Rawpixel.com/Shutterstokc.com

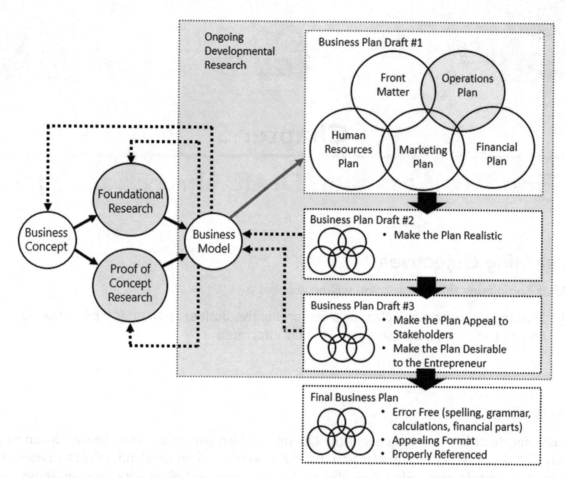

Figure 12. Operations Plan

(Illustration by Lee A. Swanson)

Operations Plan Contents

Write one to five brief introductory paragraphs to introduce the reader to what is in this section of the plan.

The Operations Plan should *inform the reader* about how the business will be structured and how it will operate. Always include well-referenced primary and secondary research results to support the plans, costs, and other information included.

The Operations Plan should answer the following key questions:

- Capacity
  - What constraints will the business operate under that will restrict its capacity to produce and sell the product?
  - Given the constraints, what is the operating capacity of the business? The operating capacity usually describes the maximum amount of production that the business can generate within a particular time frame or the maximum dollar value of sales it can generate given the operating conditions to which it will be subject (like the number of hours it can operate during a specific time).

- Workflow and Processes
  - How can the planned workflow be described or diagrammed so that readers will be satisfied that the entrepreneur has carefully and expertly thought through every element of the business operations?
  - What work will the business do and what activities will it outsource?
- Location
  - Where should the facility be located?
  - What are the zoning and other legal issues associated with the location?
  - How much will it cost to buy or lease a property at the desired location? Are there adequate facilities (buildings, parking lots, other) available at the desired location? If buying, what will be the property tax cost?
  - What parking and other costs will there be at this location (for employees and for customers)?
- Facility
  - How large will the facility be, and why must it be this size?
  - How much will it cost to buy or lease the facility? If buying, what will be the property tax cost?
  - What utility and other costs will there be for this facility?
  - What must the facility design accommodate? Should it be developed to allow for future expansion? Are there transportation and storage issues that should be accommodated?
  - What will be the facility layout, and how will this best accommodate customer and employee requirements?
- Operations Timeline
  - When will the owner register the business name, purchase equipment, and make the other preparations to start the venture?
  - When will operations begin? When will the first sale be made?
  - When might the operations need to move to a larger facility?
  - When will new product lines be offered?
  - When will new key employees be hired?
  - When will international expansion take place?
- Set up
  - What fixed assets, including equipment, machinery, furnishings, and other depreciable assets must the entrepreneur purchase before start up so the venture can conduct its business? The fixed capital requirements generally include all of the depreciable assets needed for start up and early operations. Although purchased buildings are depreciable assets, the land on which the buildings sit is not a depreciable asset. However, the land and its value should be on the list.
  - What other services or depreciable items must the business purchase before start up? Note that building renovations might or might not be depreciable depending on the jurisdiction in which the business will operate and whether the business owns the buildings being renovated.

- ○ What other expenses are necessary to prepare for business start up, including that necessary to purchase starting inventories, recruit employees, conduct market research, acquire licenses, hire lawyers, and to pay for other operational requirements before starting operations?
- Start Up
  - ○ What nonroutine or nonrecurring expenses must the company incur to meet its goals during the start up phase (after making the first sale and before the business enters the ongoing operations phase—usually over a one- to three- or four-year time span)?
- Risk Management Strategies
  - ○ To what risks is the company exposed?
  - ○ How will the risks be mitigated?
  - ○ What control processes should the entrepreneur plan to reduce the overall risks to which the company is exposed?

Operating Structure

In this section of the business plan, describe the legal structure under which the business will organize. In most jurisdictions, entrepreneurs will organize their businesses as one of the following legal forms: sole proprietorship, partnership, limited partnership, corporation, and cooperative. Explain whether the business will be organized as a for-profit or a not-for-profit enterprise, or as another type of venture, like a registered charity.

© dizain/Shutterstock.com

The financial statements, risk management strategies, and other elements of the business plan are affected by the type of legal structure chosen for the business. For example, a business plan for a partnership should include a description of the essential terms contained in the proposed partnership agreement, and the projected financial statements for a partnership will be structured slightly differently than for a corporation.

Operating Processes

This section should include a description and well–designed workflow diagram to inform readers of how the business will conduct its work. It should provide a clear indication of the planned activities for providing the goods and services to targeted customers. The workflow diagram should also satisfy targeted readers, some of whom might be experts in that type of business, that the entrepreneur fully understands how to operate the proposed venture. The challenge for business plan writers, especially when the business is of a relatively standard type, is to strike the right balance between providing enough detail to make the description and illustration of the operating processes useful for readers without being too complicated and lengthy.

While developing the detailed description of the planned operating processes, entrepreneurs should identify and address potential gaps in their plans and use their advanced workflow plan to figure out needed details such as how many workers they need and when they need them,

and what raw materials they need to order at what times. Entrepreneurs can also use the detailed workflow plan to craft strategies to distinguish themselves from competitors.

Entrepreneurs should consider whether they must implement quality improvement programs like ISO 9000 to be able to sell their products to European and other customers who might require their suppliers to have ISO 9000 certification. If this is the case, the business plan writer should indicate this in the plan and outline how the company will become certified.

Operating Capacity

The operating capacity section describes the practical maximum production level that is possible given the resources available. Business plan writers usually describe the operating capacity using a measure within a given time frame. For example, a business plan might indicate the maximum number of units the business can produce in a single day, the number of customers it can serve in a month, the number and size of contracts it can secure and complete over a defined operating season, or how many projects of various sizes it can complete in a year.

An entrepreneur can conceptualize the capacity by considering how much, at maximum, the business can produce or serve if it were to receive a significant order to fill given its current set of time, people, equipment, and other resources. So, unless there are unique restrictions beyond the physical facility and equipment limits, the maximum operating capacity for a business might be how much it could realistically produce during a month by working the regularly scheduled hours. If it is relatively easy to temporarily hire extra workers to be able to operate over extended hours, then the maximum possible production amount during the extended hours could be the capacity limitation.

Often, operating capacity can be a challenge to conceptualize and calculate. The first step is usually to determine what constraints the business faces that can restrict capacity. The usual constraints include the facility size, the type of equipment the business has, and the size and skill level of the company's available workforce. Other constraints include the type of experience the business owners want the clients to have and the hours they can operate.

Calculating the capacity can help an entrepreneur estimate the maximum sales revenue available to the company. They can then consider how close to capacity they are likely able to operate. For example, an entrepreneur might expect their firm to operate at 60% capacity over its first year of business. If so, they should explain why that is, and at what capacity level it will operate in the next years.

A company's capacity often changes as it grows or matures. When this is the case, the entrepreneur should explain the projected capacity level changes and account for them in revenue and expense projections. Capacity expansion often occurs in steps rather than in a steady upward pattern because capacity increases are usually due to new employee hires, additional machinery, or facility expansion.

Production or Merchandise Purchase Schedules

If required in a business plan, this section includes a description of the company's projected production or merchandise purchases, usually accompanied by tables showing the projections. Projected production or merchandise purchases must accommodate projected sales. They must also typically reflect a ramp–up for new businesses and seasonality patterns for most kinds of businesses that have production and sales fluctuations during the year.

Almost all new businesses have a ramp-up period during which the pattern of sales might temporarily spike during a grand opening event or when the business first opens. Sales will then typically level out at a modest rate after which the entrepreneur projects gradual sales increases as the business attracts more targeted customers and eventually starts getting repeat sales. The merchandise purchases projections should reflect the sales forecasts after the initial production run or stock–up required to have enough product available to sell at start up. Entrepreneurs must be careful to reflect a ramp-up in the pattern of production or merchandise purchases to match their projected sales.

Many businesses have seasonal sales patterns over a year. Entrepreneurs need to understand how their sales and production or merchandise purchases will be affected by seasonality and must reflect that seasonality in their projections.

Entrepreneurs should include tables in their business plan, showing their projected production or merchandise purchase schedules. When inserting tables from a financial model, usually developed in a spreadsheet template, business plan writers must ensure that all the columns and rows fit on the page without spilling over onto another page. If necessary or if it enhances the visual appeal of the business plan, writers can enhance tables with colors, lines, and other features using a consistent format throughout the plan. When desirable or needed, writers can add section breaks in their Word document to place tables on landscape formatted pages.

When including a table in a business plan, always refer to it in the text of the plan.

Location

The business plan writer should identify the exact physical location for the business if the entrepreneur has already secured it or if there is a high probability they can acquire it. In many cases, however, the physical location cannot be secured until the needed financing is in place, which might require a completed business plan. In those cases, the business plan writer should describe the facility requirements and characteristics. They can do this by using existing facilities as proxies and choosing one or more currently available locations to use to get pricing, taxation, utility costs, and other information that should be relevant at the time when the entrepreneur can secure the needed facility. For example, a business plan writer might use one available, but not necessarily ideal, property in the desired area listed by a commercial real estate company to get relevant and representative property leasing costs, or purchase and property tax costs if the plan is to buy a property. To get estimated costs for utilities, renovations, and other property-related expenses relevant to the building needed, they can use a different property listing that would reflect those needs.

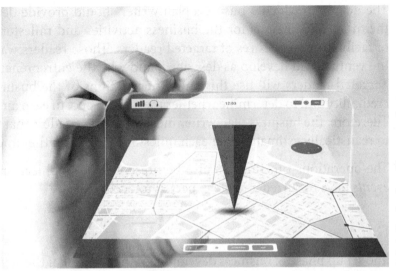

© Syda Productions/Shutterstock.com

Facilities

This section of a business plan includes information about the planned business facilities, including the desired size along with descriptions of other requirements like the building, parking, external storage, loading bays, security, and other needs.

If relevant, when including facility costs in their budgets, some business plan writers add building maintenance expenses or money for renovations and upgrades. For owned buildings, it might be appropriate to include a reserve account (like a savings plan) into which to save money for major future repairs and maintenance.

© mavo/Shutterstock.com

Business plan writers should include a diagram showing the planned facility layout. They should also address any zoning and other legal issues that might arise when securing a facility.

Operations Timeline

The degree to which a business plan writer should provide details on the time frames and explain the order and reasons for the business activities and milestones is dependent on the overall goal of facilitating the desires of targeted readers. Those readers want to fully understand how and why the venture will develop as described, and why the entrepreneur feels it will take the time outlined. Targeted readers will use this and other sections of the business plan to assess the entrepreneur's credibility and to determine whether they can expect to earn an adequate return on their investment. Therefore, the business plan writer must assure the readers that they have done the required research to realistically estimate when each milestone shown on the timeline will occur.

The operations timeline can also be presented in graphical or table form to show when *milestone events* have occurred and are expected to occur.

Set up

The set up phase of business development includes all of the activities and purchases that must occur before the business start up.

One part of the set up process includes securing all of the needed fixed capital and making all of the necessary expenditures needed to operate the business at start up. Refer to Table 1 for a partial list of activities that must occur during the start up phase. Business plan writers should include the costs associated with the relevant items from Table 1 in their business plan (see Exercise 5.2).

Table 1. Common Set up Activities

• Hire needed professionals	• Buy or lease facility
• Complete business set up (incorporate the business or finalize the partnership agreement)	• Hook up utilities
	• Get necessary building and other permits
	• Complete building renovations
• Set up business banking and money management (buy cheques, get point of sale terminals, credit card machines, other)	• Replace existing locks and get new keys cut
	• Complete other construction (like fencing, parking lot paving, and exterior lighting)
• Acquire business license	• Install indoor and outdoor signage (include design costs and time)
• Register business name	
• Register domain name	• Install needed production equipment
• Set up social media and websites	• Purchase needed office equipment and furniture (like desks, chairs, file cabinets, telephones, waiting room furniture, work tables, conference room table and chairs, curtains, decorations, staff room microwave, coffee makers, dishwasher)
• Set up customer loyalty systems	
• Purchase initial product inventory	
• Set up Internet and Wi-Fi	
• Test new facilities and processes	
• Do pre-start up advertising	
• Purchase safety equipment (like first aid kit, fire extinguishers, automated external defibrillator [AED])	• Purchase needed shelving and storage systems (including needed refrigeration equipment)
• Arrange contracts (like for janitorial services, snow removal, equipment maintenance, other)	• Install and set up computer systems (like computers, printers, scanners, copiers, all needed software, set up costs, and AV equipment)
• Pay initial membership fees (like Chamber of Commerce and professional and industry associations)	
	• Install security systems
• Recruit staff (including arranging flights, hotels, taxi rides, and meal allowances for candidates)	• Purchase insurance (like property, vehicle, liability, and key person)
	• Purchase needed supplies (like pens, paper, towels, soap, toilet paper, cleaning supplies, cutlery, plates, cooking pots, and table settings)
• Conduct initial safety training	
• Plan grand opening and other events	

Fixed Capital Requirements

The fixed capital requirements include all of the depreciable assets, including any buildings the business plans to purchase for the start up. Although land is not normally a depreciable asset, a business should include the value of planned land purchases in its fixed capital requirements list.

The business plan writer should consult catalogues from industrial suppliers to determine the prices for machinery, equipment, and furniture. It is often less costly in the long run for companies to purchase industrial quality furniture as the consumer products supplied by stores for households will likely wear out quickly when used in a commercial or industrial setting.

Often the best way to present the list of fixed capital assets that must be purchased to prepare the business for the start up is to list them in a table. If using a table, consider what level of detail is required so that the list is not too long. Sometimes, it is useful to cluster the fixed capital requirements in categories in a table.

Set Up Expenses

This section of the business plan includes the expenses needed to prepare for the start of regular operations. It should include a start up budget showing the cash required to recruit employees, conduct market research, acquire licenses, hire lawyers, and pay for the other things required before start up.

The business plan writer should consider including these expenses in a table, possibly categorized to reduce the number of items. Relevant information, including the sources for the cost figures and other information, should be included in this section—possibly in the table.

Start Up

This section includes the plans and expenses required during the start up phase. Examples include a grand opening event, introducing a new product line after a few months of operation, attending a major trade fair as a display participant, and upgrading to new equipment after cash flows are projected to be sufficient enough to pay for it.

If it improves clarity, business plan writers can include the items in this section in a table.

© Rawpixel.com/Shutterstock.com

Risk Management Strategies

The risk management section of a business plan is designed to show that the entrepreneur has considered the range of risks to which the business is exposed and how they will deal with those risks. It can improve clarity to categorize the risk exposures by those mitigated in part by insurance coverage and those dealt with through operating and management systems.

When considering the types of risks to which a venture might be exposed, it is sometimes useful to think of potential risks as those that:

1. Affect the entire enterprise, like being sued
2. Might generate financial difficulties, like not being able to secure a loan when needed or not having enough cash flow to fund planned purchases
3. Are operational, like not being able to acquire inventories when needed, having difficulty hiring the right type of employees at the right times, not making sales the company had believed were imminent, and dealing with theft, arson, and natural disasters like fires and floods.

Overall, the risk management section should describe the organization's risk exposure in simple and straight forward terms. It should also include the plans and strategies for managing each of the risks identified. The four general risk management approaches are as follows. Use these categories to help conceptualize ways to mitigate risks, but do not use these terms in a business plan.

© bleakstar/Shutterstock.com

1. Avoiding—Entrepreneurs can *avoid risks* by choosing to not do something, like choosing not to offer to deliver the products to customers.

2. Reducing—Business owners might *reduce risks* by providing training or undertaking specific operational strategies designed to improve safety.

3. Transferring—Entrepreneurs might *transfer risks* by purchasing insurance (transferring the risk of financial loss to an insurer) or outsourcing some activities (transferring the risk to a contractor).

4. Accepting (assuming)—Entrepreneurs can *accept risks* by self–insuring a vehicle fleet against physical loss. Note that they should usually purchase vehicle liability insurance to protect against loss from negligence. Vehicle owners might also accept the risk of getting a stone chip in a window by having a higher insurance deductible amount. Sometimes, entrepreneurs choose to accept risks and deal with any potential losses themselves when the costs of avoiding or transferring risks are high.

Business plan writers should organize the items in the risk management chart in a logical order. For example, they can organize the risks according to their potential of occurring. Alternatively, as shown in Table 2, the writer can organize the items in the table by how they will be mitigated. In Table 2, the mitigation categories include those that are insurable and risks that can be managed through operating systems. Another possible category is risks mitigated through management systems. If some of the mitigation strategies give rise to either monthly expenses (like monitoring costs) or capital asset needs (like remote sensing and security systems), the entrepreneur must include those purchases and expenses in the financial model.

Table 2. Example of Risk Exposure and Mitigation Table

Insurable Risks			
Risk Exposure	Risk Consequence	Risk Potential	Mitigation
Fire, flood, theft	Possibly devastating	Low	Purchase property insurance and install a security monitoring system
Lawsuit	Possibly devastating	Low	Purchase liability insurance
Owner/manager incapacitated by illness or other	Lost income and profit	Low	Purchase key person insurance
Risks Managed through Operating Systems			
Risk Exposure	Risk Consequence	Risk Potential	Mitigation
Customer payment defaults	Lost income and profit	Moderate	Credit checks, registered security, legal contracts
Customer dissatisfaction with service quality	Lost income and profit	Moderate	Provide customer service training to employees
Liability exposure when employees drive on public roads	Risk of being sued if an accident occurs	Low	Limit employee driving to picking up supplies, do not offer product delivery service to customers, provide employee driver safety training

The Risk Management Strategies section is also where an entrepreneur can describe their planned control processes. For example, they should describe how they will implement controls if employees will handle company cash or sign for supplies and inventory deliveries. Control systems might also be needed if employees communicate directly with customers, suppliers, the media, and others. It is also essential to control worker access to the company's computer systems that containing information on customers, proprietary knowledge, the financial situation, and other information only certain people should be able to access.

Chapter Summary

This chapter describes the contents of the Operations Plan part of a business plan. It covers the operating structure, processes, and capacity. The schedule for production or merchandise purchases should also be covered in this section of the plan, along with a description of the facilities and the operations timeline. Descriptions of the set up, start up, and risk management strategies also belong in the Operations Plan.

Exercises

Exercise 5.1—Write the Operations Plan

Use the Business Plan Word Template (Appendix B) to begin writing the Operations Plan.

Exercise 5.2—Develop the Financial Model Part 1

Use the Business Plan Excel Template (Appendix C) to do the following:

1. On the ControlPanel tab, fill in the company name and date that you want the financial statements to start (include the start up phase).
2. Develop the initial revenue model for years one to five on one or more of the RetailSales, ServiceSales, or ManufacturingSales tabs. Use the tab or tabs most appropriate for the business type.
3. Input the planned asset purchases (fixed capital requirements) for the first five years of the business on the AssetPurchases tab.
4. Use the Set Up tab to record the set up expenses.
5. Enter preliminary numbers and headings into the OtherExpenses tab.

Cross-Chapter Case—Tech World Pro Part 5

The Initial Operations Plan

Talia and Malik Garcia had met Greg Grandal through mutual friends, and knew that about four years ago he had started a retail store that sold home audio equipment. They decided to ask Greg for his advice on entering the retail world to sell technology-based products. Greg helped them substantially, and also introduced them to Adi and Gita Patil, who owned and operated an appliance sales and repair business.

Using their NAICS (North American Industry Classification System) code to get started, Talia and Malik found some excellent industry average revenue numbers. As that information (gleaned from secondary research) was from data reported by ongoing businesses and not start ups like theirs, the couple supplemented that information with new knowledge they acquired from Greg Grandall and Adi and Gita Patil (primary research) to project the following product sales projections.

	Year 1	Year 2	Year 3	Year 4	Year 5
Computer Repairs	120 units	25% higher	15% higher	10% higher	5% higher

Based on the advice they received, the couple does not expect any *seasonal sales patterns* on computer repairs. However, for year 1 they will not project sales in January and February when they are setting up their business.

Talia and Malik estimated that each computer repair their company does will consume, on average, $15 worth of repair-specific materials, but they have decided to build that cost into the prices. Any components or other types of supplies they need will be reflected in the next set of projections.

The couple estimated the following *annual sales in units* for each of their product categories. As shown in the table, they included a *sales ramp-up* over the first few years of operations.

	Year 1	Year 2	Year 3	Year 4	Year 5
Computer systems	152	12% higher	12% higher	7% higher	7% higher
Computer components	4,046	10% higher	10% higher	7% higher	7% higher
Computer supplies	11,966	15% higher	15% higher	8% higher	8% higher

Based on the advice Talia and Malik received from Greg, Adi, and Gita, they expected that their sales would reflect the following *seasonal sales patterns*:

- Late August and early September: 33% of annual retail sales because school starts then
- November and December: 40% of annual retail sales because of the Christmas season
- The remaining 27% of sales will be evenly distributed among the remaining months

The Garcias knew that they would have to develop a proper pricing strategy, but for the first draft of their financial model, they decided to charge their customers, on average, $100 per computer repair in year 1 and increase that amount by 5% in each of the following years.

For each of the three retail product categories, they planned to set their regular selling price at double their wholesale cost. For example, if it cost them $1,100 to purchase a computer system from their wholesaler, they planned to sell the system to their customers for double that amount, $2,200.

Based on the advice from Adi and Gita, the Garcias did not expect to extend credit to their customers until years 3, 4, and 5 when they planned to offer the following terms on 30% of the computer systems they sell: 2/10, net 30.

They did not plan to extend credit to their computer components, computer supplies, and computer repair customers.

Based on the advice from Greg and the Patils, Talia and Malik decided that they should stock their store with enough computer systems, components, and supplies to accommodate the first four months' worth of projected unit sales. Then, in each successive month, they planned to stock enough product for the next month's projected unit sales.

They estimated that the average wholesale costs would be as follows:

- Computer systems: $1,100
- Computer components: $43
- Computer supplies: $6.

The Garcias projected their wholesale costs to increase in September of year 2 in each product category by the projected consumer rate of inflation (consumer price index [CPI] rate) for that year. They expected that in September of all future years, the wholesale costs for each product category would increase by the projected CPI rate for that year. Using sound sources, like from national statistics agencies and other acknowledged forecasters, they expected the CPI rates to be as follows:

- 2023: 3.2%
- 2024: 4.0%
- 2025: 3.4%
- 2026: 2.9%.

Based on the advice they received, the Garcias believed that suppliers would be unlikely to offer Tech World Pro credit terms until year 3. At that time, they hoped that their computer systems wholesalers would provide them with the chance to purchase 40% of their stock under these terms: 2/10, net 30. In years 4 and 5, they expected vendors to offer the same terms, but for 60% of their computer systems purchases and 40% of their computer components purchases.

Talia and Malik determined that they needed to purchase the following depreciable assets during the set up phase, and pay for those assets in the months indicated below:

Depreciable Asset	Cost	Purchase Month (all during year 1)	Depreciation Rate
Land (nondepreciable)	$122,000	January	0%
Building	$2,140,000	January	4%
Building renovations (including shelving, counters, outside signage, etc.)	$225,000	January	10%
Office furniture	$28,000	February	20%
Data processing system	$8,500	February	30%
Computer equipment	$4,300	February	45%

The Garcias planned to make the following purchases during the set up phase:

Business name registration	350
Incorporation fees	680
Website domain name	120

Talia and Malik determined that they would have the following monthly expenses throughout year 1.

Outflows	Jan-2022	Feb-2022	Mar-2022	Apr-2022	May-2022	Jun-2022	Jul-2022	Aug-2022	Sep-2022	Oct-2022	Nov-2022	Dec-2022
Property Taxes	-	-	-	-	-	-	-	6,523	-	-	-	-
Property Maintenance	-	-	-	-	-	-	-	-	-	1,000	-	-
Gas, Electric, and Water Utilities	-	-	-	368	368	368	368	368	368	368	368	368
Telephones	-	85	154	154	154	154	154	154	154	154	154	154
Property and Liability Insurance	-	6,238	-	-	-	-	-	-	-	-	-	-
Business License	-	352	-	-	-	-	-	-	-	-	-	-
Professional Memberships	-	-	-	-	250	-	-	-	-	320	-	-
Professional Services	2,500	1,200	-	-	-	-	-	-	-	-	3,000	-
Banking and Transaction Costs	-	125	80	80	80	80	80	80	80	80	80	80
Cleaning and Other Supplies	-	300	-	-	-	150	-	-	-	150	-	-
Business Travel	-	-	-	-	3,500	-	-	-	-	-	-	-
Community Support	-	-	-	-	-	-	-	-	-	1,000	-	-

For year 2, they knew that they would need to directly enter the numbers shown as follows in the Excel template as opposed to using formulae to calculate them. They also planned to flag the cells in which they directly entered the numbers as *direct entry cells*, shown below as blue input cells.

Based on their research into likely cost increases for different categories of expenses, Talia and Malik planned to use the inflation factors shown in the following chart for years 2, 3, 4, and 5.

Outflows	Jan-2023	Feb-2023	Mar-2023	
Property Taxes	-	-	-	3.00%
Property Maintenance	-	-	-	5.00%
Gas, Electric, and Water Utilities	368	368	368	2.00%
Telephones	154	154	157	2.00%
Property and Liability Insurance	-	6,363	-	2.00%
Business License	-	359	-	2.00%
Professional Memberships	-	-	-	2.00%
Professional Services	-	-	-	2.00%
Banking and Transaction Costs	80	80	82	2.00%
Cleaning and Other Supplies	-	150	-	2.00%
Business Travel	-	-	-	2.00%
Community Support	-	-	-	10.00%
	-	-	-	0.00%
	-	-	-	0.00%
	-	-	-	0.00%

Cross-Chapter Case Activities—Part 5

1. Open the latest Business Plan Excel template on which you are developing the financial model for the business plan.

2. Save the Excel template using a slightly new name to reflect the current date in the first part of the file name. For example, if you completed the revision on July 3, 2021, the revised file would be named ***20210703 Tech World Pro Draft Business Plan.xlsx***.

3. Revenue Model Assumptions *on the RetailSales Worksheet*:
   - Enter the three product categories for the retail sales (do not enter the service sales numbers in this worksheet) in the blue input cells near the top of the RetailSales worksheet.
     - Hint: Enter a blank space in the unused blue input cells so that the charts below do not show the phrase "Product Category x."
   - Enter the projected sales totals in the blue input cells in Chart 2 on the RetailSales worksheet for all five years.
   - Enter the seasonal sales pattern in the blue input cells in Chart 1 on the RetailSales worksheet.
     - Hint: Use the formula *=0.33/2* in the August and September cells, *=0.40/2* in the November and December cells. As the first two months of the first year are set up months with no sales, enter zero in the January and February cells. The remaining six input cells during which the company expects to make 27% of its sales in the first year should contain this formula: *=0.27/6*. As the company will make sales during all the 12 months of years two to five, the eight months during which it expects to make 27% of its sales during those years should contain this formula: *=0.27/8*. If you use the right formulae in Chart 1, the total will end up being 100%.
   - Enter the planned stock purchases in the blue input cells in Chart 3 on the RetailSales worksheet.
     - Hint: In the February 2022 cells, use formulae to calculate the next four months' worth of projected sales. Then, in the March to November cells, use formulae to input the next month's projected sales. In the December cells, use formulae to input the next month's expected sales from the following year.
     - Hint: When you complete Chart 2 for year 2, you should be able to copy the formulae in the full block of cells directly into the blue cells for years 3, 4, and 5.
     - Hint: The December cells in year 5 will be blank because there are no forecasted sales for January of year 6, so inflate the projected purchases from December of year 4 by the increases planned for year 5 (computer systems 7%, computer components 7%, computer supplies 8%).
   - Enter the projected unit costs in the blue input cells in Chart 4 on the RetailSales worksheet.
   - Enter the projected percentage of purchases for which the company will have to pay cash in the blue input cells in Chart 5 on the RetailSales worksheet.
   - Enter the planned mark-up percentages in the blue input cells in Chart 6 on the RetailSales worksheet.
   - Enter the projected percentage of purchases for which the customers will have to pay cash (including purchases they place on their credit cards—which can be considered cash sales because the credit card companies transfer the money to you quite quickly) when they purchase the products in the blue input cells in Chart 7 on the RetailSales worksheet.

4. ***Review the CashFlows, IncomeStmts, and BalSheets worksheets*** to see how the changes you made to this point impacted the financial statements.

5. Revenue Model Assumptions *on the ServiceSales Worksheet*:
    - Enter the service product category (do not enter the product sales numbers in this worksheet) in the blue input cell near the top of the ServiceSales worksheet.
      - Hint: Enter a blank space in the unused blue input cells so that the charts below do not show the phrase "Product Category x."
    - Enter the projected sales totals in the blue input cells in Chart 2 on the ServiceSales worksheet for all five years.
    - Make sure there is no seasonal sales pattern showing in the blue input cells in Chart 1 on the ServiceSales worksheet.
      - Hint: Change the formulae in year 1 in Chart 1 to zeros for January and February and to *=1/10* for the remaining 10 months. Then, in year 2, change the cells in Chart 1 to blue input cells and enter the following formula in each of the cells from January to December: *=1/12*.
    - Enter the planned prices in the blue input cells in Chart 6 on the ServiceSales worksheet.
    - Ensure that all the blue input cells in Chart 7 on the ServiceSales worksheet indicate that you will have 100% cash collections.

6. As a retail and service firm, Tech World Pro will not generate any revenue from manufacturing activity, so *do not use the ManufacturingSales worksheet*.

7. *Review the CashFlows, IncomeStmts, and BalSheets worksheets* to see how the changes you made to this point impacted the financial statements.

8. Check your numbers by comparing your workbook to the following file: *Ch 5 World Tech Pro Sales.xlsx*.

9. Asset Purchase Assumptions *on the AssetPurchases Worksheet*.
    - Enter your planned depreciable asset purchases in the blue input cells on the AssetPurchases worksheet.

10. *Review the CashFlows, IncomeStmts, and BalSheets worksheets* to see how the changes you made to this point impacted the financial statements.

11. Check your numbers by comparing your workbook to the following file: *Ch 5 World Tech Pro Sales Assets.xlsx*.

12. Set up Assumptions *on the Set Up Worksheet*.
    - Enter the planned depreciable asset purchases in the blue input cells on the AssetPurchases worksheet.
      - Hint: The template will record those purchases and expenses as occurring during the first month showing on the financial model (January 2022), but you can change that if required.
      - Hint: You should include recurring expenses on the OtherExpenses worksheet and not on the Set Up worksheet.

13. *Review the CashFlows, IncomeStmts, and BalSheets worksheets* to see how the changes you made to this point impacted the financial statements.

14. Check your numbers by comparing your workbook to the following file: *Ch 5 World Tech Pro Sales Assets Set up.xlsx*.

15. Other Expenses Assumptions *on the OtherExpenses Worksheet*.

    • Enter the relevant expenses in the blue input cells on the OtherExpenses worksheet. When directly entering numbers into cells currently set up to populate using formulae, change the cell format to flag them as direct entry cells (format them using the blue color).

16. *Review the CashFlows, IncomeStmts, and BalSheets worksheets* to see how the changes you made to this point impacted the financial statements.

17. Check your numbers by comparing your workbook to the following file: *Ch 5 World Tech Pro Sales Assets Set up Expenses.xlsx*.

© dotshock/Shutterstock.com

Chapter 6

First Business Plan Draft: Human Resources Plan

Learning Objectives

After completing this chapter, you will be able to:

◆ Develop the human resources plan for a comprehensive business plan draft while ensuring that all parts of the business plan are fully integrated

◆ Develop the financial part of the business plan

Overview

The Human Resources Plan section of a business plan (Figure 13) outlines the organizational structure at start up and indicates what changes will occur within the first few years of operation. It then outlines the human resource needs over the first five years of operation, the recruitment strategies to secure those employees, and a description of the workplace and health and safety

© garage stock/Shutterstock.com

training the business will provide to them. This section continues with a description of the business's leadership and management strategies along with an account of how it will retain its employees. The section includes a detailed explanation of the compensation strategies and the details surrounding how much employees will be paid and why. It ends with information on the key company personnel.

Human Resources Plan Contents

The Human Resources Plan should *inform the reader* about all of the human resources–related issues and strategies. It should indicate precisely how many employees are needed and when. This part of the plan should inform the reader about how much the company will pay each employee while justifying the rates indicated and explaining all the benefits the firm will provide to workers. It should explain how the entrepreneur will manage human resources.

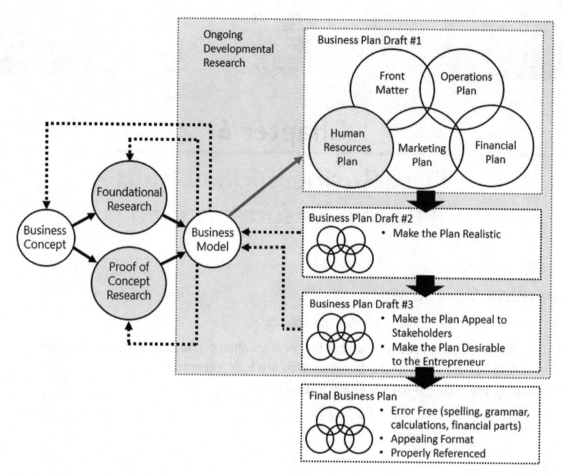

Figure 13. Human Resources Plan

(Illustration by Lee A. Swanson)

As with all parts of the business plan, the facts, amounts, and other information presented in the human resources plan must be supported by well-referenced primary and secondary research results.

The Human Resources Plan should answer the following key questions:

- Structure
  - How will the company's organizational chart be structured at start up? How will it change over the first few years of operation?
  - Why are those the best structures for the company?
- Human Resource Needs
  - What are the key positions within the organization?
  - How many employees will the company need (and have), and why?
  - What characteristics define the desired employees?
- Recruitment Strategies
  - What recruitment strategies will the business apply? What processes will the entrepreneur apply to hire the needed employees?

- Training and Health and Safety
    - What employee development methods will the company apply?
    - What health and safety training is required by law? How will the business make sure its employees have this training?
    - What additional health and safety training will the company provide?
    - Who will deliver the needed training?
    - How much will the training cost the company?
- Leadership and Management
    - What is the desired corporate culture?
    - What is the leadership strategy, and why has the entrepreneur chosen that approach? How does it align with the stated company values? How will the entrepreneur ensure those leadership methods are applied consistently and management methods are applied effectively throughout the organization?
- Retention
    - What retention strategies will the company use?
- Performance Appraisal System
    - What is the performance appraisal strategy? What performance appraisal system will the company apply?
    - Will the performance appraisal system allow for both formative and summative evaluations?
    - How will the company deal with employees who are not performing well?
    - Will the performance appraisal system be used to make compensation and job advancement decisions? If so, how?
- Compensation
    - How will each employee be paid—wage, salary, commission, other methods—and how much will they be paid?
    - What are the payroll costs, including benefits?
- Key Personnel
    - Who are the key people in the business, and what are their backgrounds?
    - If the company has more than one owner, how will profits and responsibilities be divided between the owners?
    - If the company is a partnership, have the owners agreed on a detailed partnership agreement? If so, what are the terms of the partnership (a sample partnership agreement outlining the crucial terms can be included as a business plan appendix).
    - Will the owners have key–person insurance coverage?

Organizational Structure

The organizational structure part of the business plan should include a figure showing the business's structure at start up, with some accompanying dialogue explaining the structure. The explanations can include what functions each of the positions on the organizational chart will fulfill. If the people who will fill positions are known, include their names on the figure.

© Syda Productions/Shutterstock.com

This section often includes an organizational chart, or charts, showing new company configurations that the owner expects to be in place at different stages of business development during the first five years of operations. These charts inform targeted readers of the expected changes to the human resource needs as the business develops. Provide written explanations of the changes. If it adds value, direct readers to parts of the Operations Plan that detail the expected business growth to clarify any human resource changes shown in the additional charts.

This section might include information on an Advisory Board or a Board of Directors from which the company will seek advice, guidance, or direction. Generally, an Advisory Board provides advice to the company's leaders or management team whereas a Board of Directors has authority to direct the leaders and management team—and might have the responsibility to hire and fire the leaders. So, an Advisory Board will be depicted differently on an organization chart than will a Board of Directors.

Human Resource Needs

In this section of the plan, explain all of the human resources needs in terms of exactly how many employees the business needs, what types of employees the firm needs, when the business needs them, and why they are needed. The human resource needs will often change as the business develops, so describe the requirements at start up and when changes are planned throughout the business plan's five–year scope.

Provide employee profiles for the different categories of workers the business needs, but avoid replicating information provided in the Key Personnel section. If the employee profiles fit better under the Compensation or Recruitment Strategies sections, place them there instead.

If the business plans to employ hourly-paid, part-time, or contract workers, a detailed standard weekly or monthly employee work schedule will be required to help the business plan writer figure out human resource and recruitment needs and payroll calculations. This schedule can reside in this section, or one of the Compensation or Recruitment Strategies sections.

Recruitment Strategies

© mavo/Shutterstock.com

Describe the recruitment strategies, including the sources for recruitment, the processes, and the estimated costs and timelines. For example, the recruitment process might include the following steps:

1. Assemble a hiring committee of the general manager plus two key employees
2. Develop a job profile
3. Place ads in targeted places like LinkedIn
4. Screen applicants
5. Invite shortlisted candidates for interviews and inform the others that they are not being invited to an interview
6. Interview the shortlisted candidates
7. Offer the position to the top candidate, if there is one, otherwise seek new applicants
8. Inform the remaining shortlisted candidates that the position is filled *after the top candidate accepts*—or offer the position to the next top candidate if the first one declines
9. Implement onboarding processes for the new hire

The recruitment costs might include the following, and must be included in the financial model:

1. Employment ad costs
2. Interview costs to reimburse to candidates
   a. Transportation (flights, car rental, taxi services, and other) subject to approved airline passenger categories and other criteria
   b. Accommodations
   c. Per diem for up to three days

3. interview costs

   a. Employee time to arrange employment ads, head–hunter meetings, candidate transportation, accommodations, record keeping for reimbursement, and setting up interview rooms and times, company tour, city tour, city housing tour with real estate agent, and meals with company employees

4. New hire signing bonus, relocation, training, and other onboarding costs

Sometimes, it is desirable and most cost-effective to try to recruit an appealing candidate from a competitor and then implement robust retention strategies (described in the Retention Strategies section of the business plan).

In many cases, ventures start without the need to hire staff since the entrepreneur, possibly with a partner or spouse, might run the business until employees are needed. In that case, entrepreneurs should explain this and describe how they can operate the business with the planned human resources. They should explain how they plan to deal with illnesses, vacations, and other situations that might leave their business unattended if they do not have a contingency plan. They should also consider situations like if their business is in a shopping mall that requires all leaseholders to be operational when the mall is open.

Training

This section of the business plan describes the required and planned employee training activities. Some training might be required by law or by professional associations, and other training might be optional but might provide the business with payback in terms of productivity or risk mitigation.

Parts of the training program might be designed for new employees, like orientation programs and equipment training. Other parts of the training program might include annual or more frequent instruction for existing employees.

© Stock Rocket/Shutterstock.com

Some training requirements might be paid for by the company, and might also include time off from regular work commitments to attend training sessions to help them become more effective supervisors or salespeople. In this case, the business must plan how to cover the work those employees cannot do when they are training. The business might require employees to do some training on their own time and at their own cost as a condition of employment.

In all cases, the business plan writer must indicate to readers that they are aware of, and have developed plans to accommodate all applicable employment laws for their jurisdiction. They should also demonstrate their awareness of all other employment considerations, like union issues and the health and safety concerns addressed in the Health and Safety section (described next).

Health and Safety

The Health and Safety section of a business plan outlines a business's plans and strategies for ensuring its workers have the needed information, equipment, and supplies to keep the workplace safe. Some jurisdictions have laws in place that require all employees to have training on topics like workplace hazardous materials handling and how to drive forklifts. Some businesses choose to provide additional training for things like first aid, automated external defibrillators (AEDs), and driver training education for employees that might require drivers' license endorsements for large trucks with air brakes.

© Garsya/Shutterstock.com

Leadership and Management Strategies

In this section of the business plan, entrepreneurs should describe their leadership and management strategies. They should demonstrate that they have considered different formal leadership styles and have chosen to implement one that best fits the workplace context. Business plan writers should draw from academic research and tested practitioner methods to implement leadership styles and management strategies best suited to their business type.

© Rawpixel.com/Shutterstock.com

The leadership style chosen should align with the stated values and help develop the desired operating culture. It is not good enough in a business plan for entrepreneurs to state what they want to achieve—like having the best work environment, an appealing organizational culture, and a diversified workplace—without describing why they want those outcomes and how they will achieve them.

Retention Strategies

It is generally considered to be much more cost-effective to implement retention strategies to retain valued employees than to lose them and have to recruit and train new workers and wait until they have gained enough experience to match the productivity levels of those who left. Use this section of the business plan to describe the business's retention strategies. While retention is often associated with compensation strategies, it might have as much or more to do with operational strategies to ensure job satisfaction and provide advancement opportunities where and when possible.

The retention strategies and performance appraisal system should be connected because a sound performance appraisal system can contribute to job satisfaction, and might also be linked to pay increases. The Performance Appraisal System section is described next.

Performance Appraisal System

This section of the business plan should describe a full performance appraisal system, not just a performance appraisal instrument or meeting that occurs periodically. A Performance Appraisal System involves a persistent approach to making sure that employees always understand how their employer feels about their job performance, and methods to, where possible, help them continually improve their job performance.

The business plan writer should provide details about how the entrepreneur plans to set up the system and why the chosen approach is optimal for the business. They should describe what outcomes they expect from the performance appraisal system besides the employees learning about how the employer feels about their performance. These systems should be *formative* by providing honest feedback to employees to help them continually improve in their work and to help the employer understand what can be done to help them improve.

Performance appraisal system should also outline how and when the business will conduct *summative* appraisals when an employee has established a record of substandard performance despite the company's documented efforts to help them improve their performance or conduct. Summative evaluations prescribe corrective actions, often supported by training for the employee and supervisor help to promote improved performance, which will result in dismissal if specific improvements in performance do not occur within a reasonable amount of time.

When developing a performance appraisal system, the entrepreneur should decide whether it will support employee pay raises and job advancement decisions. If so, the entrepreneur should carefully design the performance appraisal system to ensure that it fairly, and in a transparent way, provides the needed outputs to support compensation or advancement decisions.

Compensation

Use this section of the plan to explain the business's compensation strategies. Indicate how much the company will pay each employee or employee category, and why it will pay that amount. Justify the rates paid by comparing them to the applicable average market rates found through research agencies. The business plan writer should explain how they used the average market wage and salary rates when determining how much to pay the employees.

Include all payroll benefits required by law in the compensation calculations. Also, include all benefits that the company voluntarily offers to its employees, like pension and dental plans and additional vacation time.

The compensation strategy should ensure both internal and external pay equity. Owners must carefully plan any incentive-based pay or profit-sharing systems they wish to offer to employees.

© Andrey_Popov/Shutterstock.com

Key Personnel

Entrepreneurs can include brief biographies for themselves and selected key employees, and perhaps others—like mentors or business coaches—in this part of the business plan. The purpose of this section is to inform targeted readers about the unique skill sets, education, experience, and other factors that will help ensure business success.

Chapter Summary

This chapter described the essential elements of the Human Resources Plan section of the business plan. It described the contents of the organizational structure, human resource needs, recruitment strategies, training, leadership and management strategies, retention strategies, performance appraisal, compensation strategies, and key personal sections of the business plan.

Exercises

Exercise 6.1—Write the Human Resources Plan

Use the Business Plan Word Template (Appendix B) to begin writing the Human Resources Plan.

Exercise 6.2—Develop the Financial Model Part 2

Use the Business Plan Excel Template (Appendix C) to do the following:

1. On the Employees tab, add the relevant percentages in the four payroll deduction fields near the top of the worksheet.
2. On the Employees tab, fill in the number of salary and wage employees the company will need over the five–year time frame along with the average annual salary the salaried employees will be paid and the average wage rate all wage employees will earn. Add the average hours per wage earner for each month.
3. If relevant, on the Contractors tab, fill in the number of contractors (nonemployees) along with the average amount they will be paid in each month during the five years covered by the business plan when the company will hire contractors to do some work.
4. Enter more numbers and headings into the OtherExpenses tab.

Cross-Chapter Case—Tech World Pro Part 6

The Initial Human Resources Plan

Talia and Malik Garcia have determined that they need to employ one salaried person starting in February of year 1 at a rate of $45,000 per year plus legislated benefits as follows:

- Employment insurance—1.88%
- Government pension plan—4.95%
- Workers' compensation—3.12%.

They plan to increase the salary rate by 5% in February of years 2 and 3.

In August of year 3, the couple plans to hire a second salaried employee, and because they will pay the new employee less than the existing one, the average salary rate will drop to $46,153.

In February of year 4 the average rate will increase by 3% and again by 5% in February of year 5.

Additionally, they plan to employ two half-time wage employees in February of year 1 at an average wage rate of $12.52. Those half-time employees will each work 80 hours per month.

The legislated benefit rates are the same as for the salary workers plus holiday pay at a rate of 5%.

The wage employee hiring plan will be to have two half-time workers (each working 80 hours per month) from January to July, then to have five half-time workers (also each working 80 hours per month) in August, September, November, and December. In October, which is between the two peak sales seasons, the Garcias will have three half-time wage employees each working 80 hours per month.

They plan to increase the average wage rate by 3% each August, starting in year 2.

Talia and Malik have determined that they need to hire one contract person to help with business set up and training in February of year 1. They will hire that person for 50 hours at a rate of $125 per hour.

Cross-Chapter Case Activities—Part 6

1. Open the latest Business Plan Excel Template on which you are developing the financial model for the business plan.

2. Save the Excel template using a slightly new name to reflect the current date in the first part of the file name. For example, if you completed the revision on July 10, 2021, the revised file would be named *20210710 Tech World Pro Draft Business Plan.xlsx*.

3. Employees Assumptions *on the Employees Worksheet*:

   - Enter the relevant payroll deductions in the blue input cells on the Employees worksheet.

   - Enter the employee assumptions (numbers of salary employees, average annual salary amounts, numbers of wage employees, average wage rates, and average hours per wage earner) in the blue input cells for years 1 to 5 on the Employees worksheet.

     ○ Note: The Employees Worksheet also contains fields for inputting the costs for four discretionary human resource costs the company will incur if its strategies call for additional benefits and training allowances: retirement plan contributions, health benefits contributions, training allowance costs, and bonus pay.

4. Contractors Assumptions *on the Contractors Worksheet*:
   - Enter the relevant contractor assumptions in the blue input cells on the Contractors worksheet.
5. *Review the CashFlows, IncomeStmts, and BalSheets worksheets* to see how the changes you made to this point impacted the financial statements.
6. Check your numbers by comparing your workbook to the following file: *Ch 6 World Tech Pro Employees Contractors.xlsx*.

© dotshock/Shutterstock.com

Chapter 7

First Business Plan Draft: Marketing Plan

Learning Objectives

After completing this chapter, you will be able to:

◆ Develop the marketing plan for a comprehensive business plan draft while ensuring that all parts of the business plan are fully integrated

◆ Develop the financial part of the business plan

Overview

The Marketing Plan section of a business plan (Figure 14) includes the results of primary and secondary research and analysis *relevant to the venture*. That research and analysis is categorized under the market, competitive, and organizational categories. The target market is then described along with target customer profiles, if relevant.

© Rawpixel.com/Shutterstock.com

This part of the business plan includes detailed descriptions of the product, pricing, distribution, and promotions strategies. As strategies, each of those subsections contain plans of action designed to achieve specific goals. The plans of action must be backed up with evidence or strong arguments that they will help the company meet its goals. The strategies give rise to resource needs and the costs reflected in the financial model.

The Marketing Plan section ends with sales schedules that indicate at least five years worth of sales projections.

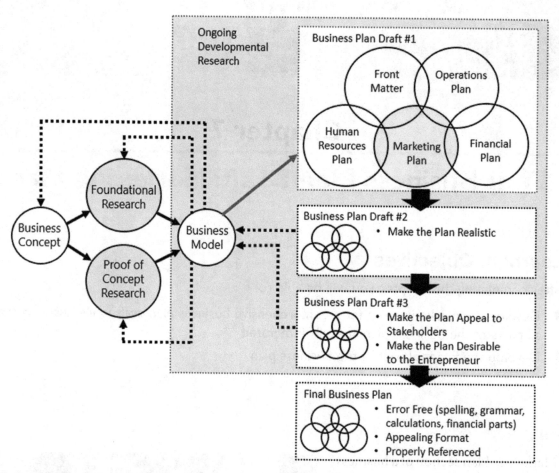

Figure 14. Marketing Plan

(Illustration by Lee A. Swanson)

Marketing Plan Contents

Targeted business plan readers will use the Marketing Plan to learn about the strategies developed by the company, and backed up by valid primary and secondary research and solid arguments, to ensure the business sells enough of its products and services to thrive. It also contains the projected sales schedules that are part of the financial model used to develop the projected financial statements that help the business plan writer continually revise plans to make the venture ever more financially sustainable and appealing to investors.

Business plan writers should assume that targeted readers, especially those considering investing their money in the business, will naturally question the assumptions the writer made. They will initially assume the planned time frames are too long, revenues overstated, and expenses underestimated. To counter these assumptions and provide readers with solid reasons to trust the plan contents, writers must supply well-crafted explanations and back up all the numbers in the plan.

The Marketing Plan should answer the following key questions:

- Market Analysis
  - Will it be evident to targeted readers that the Market Analysis is based on valid market research outcomes?
  - Does the Market Analysis describe the current and projected economic conditions that will impact the target customers' ability and willingness to purchase the company's products?
- Competitive Analysis
  - Who are the business's competitors? Is it important to consider both direct and indirect competitors when developing strategies to attract targeted customer to this business?
  - What is the company's competitive advantage?
  - What distinguishes the business from that of competitors?
- Organizational Analysis
  - What are the strengths and weaknesses of the organization?
  - What strategies should the business implement to take advantage of strengths and mitigate weaknesses?
  - What strategies should the business implement to take advantage of available opportunities and to mitigate threats?
  - What skill sets do the entrepreneur and the key employees bring to the business? What gaps are there in the skill sets?
  - Does the company have adequate financial resources available to run the business, manage cash flows, and deal with unexpected events?
- Target Market
  - Who are the best potential customers for the business to pursue?
  - Are those targeted customers identifiable and reachable?
  - How do those people make purchase decisions for products or services like those the company sells?
- Target Customer Profile
  - What demographic, psychographic, geographic, behavioral, and other characteristics define the target customers?
- Marketing Strategy
  - What is the optimum marketing mix?
  - Why is that marketing mix better than the alternatives?
  - Is part of the marketing strategy to establish an appealing brand?
- Product Strategy
  - What is the proposed product mix (the products and services the company intends to sell)? In what way does this product mix choice constitute a well-thought-out product strategy?
  - In what ways will the proposed product mix appeal to targeted customers better than the alternatives available to them?

- If the product mix is composed of standardized products, on what basis will the company compete? Will it offer more appealing prices than those of competitors? Will it offer something else to appeal to targeted customers, like a superior location, better customer service, better quality, more features, or an appealing style?
- Pricing Strategy
  - What makes the planned pricing strategies better than the alternatives?
- Distribution Strategy
  - What makes the planned distribution strategies better than the alternatives?
- Promotions Strategy
  - In what ways will the business communicate with its targeted customers?
  - What messages will the company convey to targeted customers?
  - How much will the promotions plan cost?
  - As a new entrant into the market, must the business attract customers away from competitors or will it create new customers for its products and services?
  - If it wants to attract customers away from competitors, how will those rivals respond to the threat?
  - If it wants to create new customers, how will it convince them to reallocate their dollars toward the business's products and services and away from other things they want to purchase?
- Sales Schedules
  - What are the company's sales forecasts over the five years covered by the business plan?
  - What facts and assumptions did the business plan writer use to estimate sales?

Market Analysis

This section of a business plan provides targeted readers with a full description of the market the company is entering, including how the current and forecast economic and industry conditions might impact it. More importantly, the research work required to understand the market provides the business plan writer with the information required to define the target market and develop strategies to meet its needs in a way that can help the company succeed. As an *analysis*, this section uses available information, and possibly some stated assumptions, to draw conclusions about the current and future state of the market.

A first step to analyzing the market is to define it. When analyzing the defined market, the business plan writer should simultaneously figure out what the target market is as a subset of the overall market composed of the potential customers to whom it is most desirable to try to sell the company's products and services.

The information in this section complements that in the Business Need part of the Introduction. The purpose of the Business Need section is to prove as much as possible that there is a need for the business. The purpose of the Market Analysis is to present research analyses to use when determining the target market and developing the marketing strategy. The writer should demonstrate to targeted readers that they not only understand the operating environment within the market but that they have figured out how best to operate the business within that market.

Business plan writers must show evidence of having conducted useful primary and secondary research (see Chapter 2 and use the Research Analysis Worksheets in Appendix A). They must be careful to back up all statements of fact with properly referenced supporting evidence. A writer must indicate it if they based a claim on an assumption instead of a fact, and explain how they used the assumption to draw a conclusion.

The market analysis should include an assessment of the current and forecast economic, legal, and other conditions (PESTEL [political, economic, social, technological, environmental, and legal] Analysis), the state of the industry in which the business resides (Five Forces Model), and an assessment of the market factors (5C Market Analysis and Market Profile Analysis) as described in Chapter 2 and supported by the worksheets in Appendix A. The conclusions from the analyses should support strategy development. Strategies should be designed to overcome identified and forecast challenges and take advantage of potential opportunities.

Competitive Analysis

The market analysis and competitive analysis are closely related in that the market analysis helps readers understand the pertinent features of the market. Until they know that, a competitive analysis will be less meaningful. Both are *analyses* in that they go beyond presenting information to using it to draw conclusions about the current and future state of the market and the competitive environment within it.

© Constantin Stanciu/Shutterstock.com

The competitive analysis examines—using both primary and secondary research results (see Chapter 2 and use the Research Analysis Worksheets in Appendix A)—the current and projected future competitive environment in which the business will operate. It includes information on the individual direct competitors within a defined area unless there are too many of them in which case it will examine the main competitors individually and the rest grouped into relevant categories. If relevant, it also includes information on indirect competitors.

When doing a competitive analysis, use the appropriate tools (PESTEL, Five Forces Model, 5C Market Analysis and Market Profile Analysis—see Chapter 2 and Appendix A) to assess the competitive environment at the societal, industry, and market levels of analysis.

When writing this part of the plan, the entrepreneur should prove that they have anticipated the competitor responses to the business entrance into the market, especially if business success depends on winning customers away from those businesses. They should provide a detailed description of the competitors, including an analysis of their strengths and weaknesses and their likely response to this business's entry into the market.

A concern with doing competitive analyses is that there is no real middle ground. An entrepreneur must either analyze the entire competitive environment or clearly define and analyze the particular segment of the environment in which their business will compete. The danger lies in leaving a reader with an impression that the competitive analysis is incomplete. The writer must ensure that the competitive analysis is comprehensive (for the entire competitive landscape or a defined segment of it) and that the reader will understand that it is complete.

Some businesses might have direct and indirect competitors, where direct competitors sell primarily the same products or services and indirect competitors sell different products or services that satisfy the same basic customer want or need. The relevance is that some kinds of companies have to be concerned about direct competitors, and others have to also worry about indirect competitors when competing for customer dollars.

The business plan writer should consider including a positioning (or perceptual) map to show where the product will be positioned relative to competitors' products. They should also consider including a competitor analysis table in which competitors are rated on a set of factors to establish a competitive score against which to compare competitors. See the Word Template (Appendix B) for examples of a positioning map and a competitor analysis table.

Organizational Analysis

Like with other *analysis* sections of the plan, the goal is to present an organizational analysis that does more than present information on the business—whether existing or still being planned. To make this section of the plan an *analysis*, it should draw conclusions about the current and future state of the business. Most of the analysis in this section will be at the organizational level and will apply tools like a SWOT/TOWS Analysis, Financial Projections

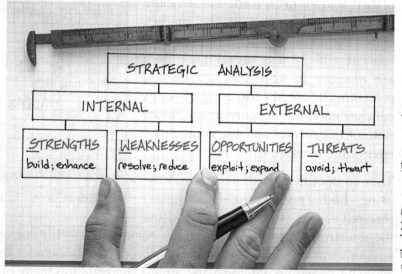

© Chad McDermott/Shutterstock.com

and Analysis, Founder Fit Analysis, and Core Competency Analysis (see Chapter 2 and use the Research Analysis Worksheets in Appendix A).

Target Market

© Jirsak/Shutterstock.com

Define the target market by identifiable groups of people who share common characteristics and who can make or significantly influence buying decisions. For example, it is not meaningful for a company to indicate that it is targeting universities. Instead, it could define its target market as female university students between the ages of 18 and 25 who are enrolled at Canadian universities. Alternatively, it might target information technology managers employed at midwestern American universities or student leaders at Mexican universities.

The target market should be defined before developing the strategies and plans for the marketing mix—including the product and service, distribution, promotional, and pricing strategies—because the strategies should be developed for the target market. In the end, the defined target market must align completely with all elements of the marketing mix. If it does not, the entrepreneur needs to either choose a different target market or adjust the marketing mix to the needs of the target market. For example, if the defined target market is female Canadian university students between the ages of 18 and 25, the product component of the marketing mix should be something that appeals to that target market.

The business plan writer must use all available research—primary and secondary—to figure out how the targeted customers make their buying decisions so they can develop the optimum mix of pricing, distribution, promotions, and product decisions to best appeal to the targeted customers.

The writer should also provide a strong justification for targeting potential customers. Reasons for targeting specific identifiable groups, beyond their stated or expected desire to purchase the product or service, includes the ability to reach them in cost-effective ways, the likelihood of being able to convince them to purchase the product or service, and the opportunity to persuade them to switch from purchasing from competitors to buying from the new business.

When defining a target market, an entrepreneur needs to figure out how to segment potential customers based on how they decide to purchase the product or service. They should target customers using one or a combination of the following segmentation methods:

- Psychographic segmentation (how people think)
    - Sets of activities or interests, for example,
        - Sports–minded versus not
        - Music–minded versus not
        - The desire to spend time in the outdoors versus preferring to stay in the city
        - Loving reading versus not reading much
    - Opinions, for example,
        - Liberal-minded versus conservative
        - Believing that branded products are better than generic
    - Lifestyles, for example,
        - Preferring to work longer hours versus enjoying more free time
        - Being more physically active versus less
    - Personality, for example,
        - Introverted versus extroverted
        - Fashion-conscious versus not caring much about fashion
    - Values, for example,
        - Valuing family time versus preferring to spend time with friends or alone
        - Politically active versus less involved in politics
        - Volunteering versus not volunteering much
- Demographic segmentation (population characteristics)
    - Age (or generational characteristics—baby boomers versus millennials)
    - Gender
    - Education
    - Occupation
    - Income level
    - Ethnicity
    - Married or not
- Geographic segmentation
    - Where people live or travel (cities, regions, neighborhoods)
    - Geographic characteristics (cold versus warm climates, rainy versus dry regions, rural versus urban, densely versus sparsely populated)
- Behavioral segmentation
    - Early adopters versus prefer to purchase after a product has been around for a while
    - Become loyal to a brand or company versus buy because of price or other factors
    - Tend to purchase green products versus choosing the lowest price products

Business plan writers often make the mistake of reverting to a simple demographic and geographic segmentation rather than targeting better and more lucrative segments. It can be tempting to try to reach people within a certain age range who are in a particular income bracket (demographic segmentation) and who live in a particular area (geographic segmentation). However, the business might benefit more by refining that target market to include psychographic and behavioral characteristics. With better customer targeting, a business can develop better marketing strategies.

Target Customer Profiles

Target customer profiles are descriptions of people (often fictional but highly realistic) that fit within the target market and, together, provide the reader with a better understanding of the range of people whom the business has chosen to target and why it has chosen that target market. The writer should describe several target customer profiles to help describe the chosen target market.

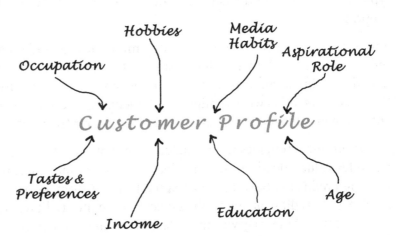

Target customer profiles provide business plan writers with a way to personalize business plan pitches and make it easier for targeted readers and potential investors to understand the target market and why the proposed marketing strategies should generate the desired results.

Marketing Strategy

Strategies are plans of action for achieving predetermined goals. This section of a business plan presents strategies for achieving marketing goals. So, to develop this section, the entrepreneur must first establish marketing goals. The following subsections detail the marketing mix strategies; those that fall under the product, pricing, distribution, and promotion categories.

In this part of the business plan, introduce the marketing strategies using one or a few introductory paragraphs. It is also in this part where the writer should detail the general marketing goals and the marketing strategies that do not fall under any of the following subsections.

Product Strategy

The product strategy is designed to achieve goals related to the product or service the company will deliver to customers. The strategies should include descriptions of the actions the company plans to take to ensure that the product or service meets the target market needs such that the targeted customers will be willing to pay the prices the entrepreneur plans to charge them. The product strategy might include plans for establishing or improving product or service quality levels to match or exceed those of the competition. If relevant, it should also detail the strategies for further product development and after-sales service. Often it is in this section where the entrepreneur describes the types and range of products the business intends to deliver to customers, and why this product mix is optimal.

The description of the product strategy might also include information on the ordering system if the business has a better system than existing competitors. The entrepreneur needs to determine how the business can provide the most convenient, easy–to–use, and responsive ordering system to the customers, otherwise, it might be challenging to convince them to switch their allegiance to the entrepreneur's business from whomever they currently purchase the product or service.

Other product strategies might include descriptions of when, how, why, and to whom the business will offer value-added services like installation, maintenance, warranties, returns, and credit. When offering credit, the business must agree to let customers pay for the product or service after they receive it. A credit strategy involves determining the credit terms, like 2/10, net 30 (customer receives a 2% discount if they pay within 10 days of purchase; otherwise they must pay within 30 days, or they have to pay interest charges on the outstanding balance on their bill). A credit strategy also includes other details, like how the business will determine to whom to extend credit.

When explaining the product strategy, resist the temptation to claim that the business will provide a superior product or service compared to the existing competitors. While that might be the goal, the only meaningful judge of success in this regard will be customers. Making such a claim might also imply to readers that the entrepreneur underestimates the wisdom, experience, and market knowledge the competitors have. If the entrepreneur has robust research outcomes indicating targeted customers are dissatisfied with the products and services provided by existing competitors, and the research indicates how the business can provide the products and services customers want and how it can attract them to the business from the competitors, they need to explain this to readers in this section.

If the product or service is standardized, the business might need to compete on price, having a superior location, better branding, superior selection, or improved service. If this is the case, describe those strategies in this section of the business plan.

Pricing Strategy

In this section, describe what the product and service prices will be and why those are the optimum rates. Entrepreneurs should base their prices on one or more established pricing strategies, like economy, premium, cost–plus, price skimming, penetration, competitive, value-based, discriminatory, bundle, promotional, and captive pricing strategies.

The entrepreneur should describe in this section of the plan the more detailed strategies related to pricing, including strategies that might include plans to accept payment by credit card (which is probably a necessity for most companies), and through online and other means.

Pricing strategies that include providing customers with the ability to pay by credit card gives rise to costs. There might be costs to acquire the equipment required to accept credit card and debit card payments, and there might be transaction fees (which can be up to 2% to 3% of the sale amount) charged every time a customer uses the credit card machine. Of course, those fees must be included in the financial model when forecasting revenues and expenses. One way to do this is to explain that the prices used in revenue calculations are the amount the business gets, and customers pay more than that to cover the credit card fees. Another way to do this is to include a cost of sales line for credit card transaction charges and then to include those charges in the prices. The second method provides more information to readers because the charges are not hidden; however, the first method might be easier to include in a financial model and is acceptable if accompanied by an explanation.

The chosen pricing strategies must be reflected in the revenue calculations shown in the sales schedules included later in the marketing plan.

Distribution Strategy

Distribution strategies include any planned methods to provide the products and services to customers, including through retail outlets, online sales, catalogue sales, salespeople, and wholesalers. When describing these strategies, business plan writers must detail all of the associated costs.

When the main, or only distribution strategy is to sell products through a retail outlet, there seems like little to include in this section. In those cases, entrepreneurs can describe their service strategies in this part of the plan. Service strategy might also be described in the product strategy or human resources strategy sections if it makes more sense to cover them there. Service strategy descriptions can explain things like the protocols staff will use when greeting customers and providing postsale follow-ups (which might mean including customer service training for staff in the Human Resources Plan).

If not included in the Product Strategies section, planned actions for packaging the product might be included under Distribution Strategies, especially if the plans include packaging differently for some of the targeted customers—maybe by including a personalized message, new product offers, or other things of value to targeted customers. Whether in this section of the plan or under product strategies, the entrepreneur must remember to include information on the packaging costs.

Promotions Strategy

Promotional strategies include plans about how to convince potential customers in the most cost-effective way to purchase the business's products and services. Sometimes, this involves advertising using methods like sponsored online or social media ads, newspaper ads, promotional pamphlets, business cards, and telephone directories. It might also include other methods, like sponsorships (like purchasing uniforms for a little league soccer team), distributing personalized pens and other promotional items to potential customers, donating items to charity auctions, mailing or electronically distributing holiday greetings or birthday wishes to potential clients, and joining organizations like the local chamber of commerce. Businesses might also participate as a presenter at trade fairs to directly reach potential customers. Some businesses have salespeople to make personal sales. The promotional strategy includes planning the optimum promotional mix from those and other methods for communicating with potential customers or otherwise making them aware of the business and what it offers to them.

A new entrant into the market must either attract customers away from the suppliers they currently buy from or create new customers for their products or services. New businesses that plan to attract customers away from competitors must consider how those rivals will respond to the threat posed by the new market entry. Businesses planning to create new customers have to convince them to reallocate their dollars from whatever the customers currently spend that money on. The promotional strategies must reflect the decisions made about where customers will be acquired.

Business plan writers must consider which promotional strategies to use. While using a medium like television may initially sound appealing, it is expensive even when running ads during non–prime times. Entrepreneurs considering this type of advertising medium must do a cost-benefit analysis to be sure they are spending their money in the best way possible.

Promotional planning includes determining all of the costs associated with implementing the planned promotional methods. Review the Business Plan Word Template (Appendix B) for an example of a table that can be included in a business plan to illustrate the promotional plan for a business. Some entrepreneurs add discretionary money to their promotional budgets to have it available if appealing promotional opportunities arise during the year.

Sales Schedules

This section of a business plan should include a description of the sales projections along with tables showing the projections. Sales projections for new businesses should reflect a ramp-up period when the business first opens and sales might be temporarily higher or when it holds a grand opening event. Sales then tend to decline to a modest level as the business strives to attract new customers and eventually earn customer loyalty to get repeat sales. Entrepreneurs will then project gradual sales increases.

The sales projections for almost all kinds of companies should also show seasonality patterns. Entrepreneurs must understand how their sales will be affected by seasonality and reflect those patterns in their yearly sales projections.

When inserting tables from a financial model developed in a spreadsheet, business plan writers should make sure that all the columns and rows fit on a single page.

Business plan writers should make monthly sales forecasts and link them directly to the projected cash flow statements. They need to explain any assumptions they make, and provide references for the information they got from sources. Use the Business Plan Excel Template (Appendix C) to develop the financial model, including the sales projections.

Chapter Summary

This chapter summarized the elements of the Marketing plan part of the business plan. It covered the market, competitive, and organizational analysis sections while highlighting that they must be research-based and draw conclusions upon which strategies can be developed. This chapter also introduced the target market and target customer profile parts of a business plan. It then described the marketing strategy section, including its product, pricing, distribution, and promotions strategy subsections. The chapter finished by describing the sales schedules and how they should reflect a sales ramp-up and seasonality.

Exercises

Exercise 7.1—Write the Marketing Plan

Use the Business Plan Word Template (Appendix B) to begin writing the Marketing Plan.

Exercise 7.2—Develop the Financial Model Part 3

Use the Business Plan Excel Template (Appendix C) to do the following:

1. Review the revenue model developed as part of Exercise 5.2 and update it as needed.
2. On the Promotions tab, replace the example promotional methods with the methods the company will use.
3. On the same tab, fill in the costs for each promotional method for each month over the five-year time frame.

Cross-Chapter Case—Tech World Pro Part 7

The Initial Marketing Plan

Based on their research, Talia and Malik have determined that they will make the following promotions expenditures during year 1.

	Feb-2022	Mar-2022	Jun-2022	Jul-2022	Aug-2022	Nov-2022
ABC Printers - posters	965	-	-	-	-	-
ABC Printers - Business cards	59	-	-	59	-	59
Daily XYZ Newspaper	668	-	-	-	1,121	2,117
Grand opening and sales events	-	2,858	-	-	1,215	-
Website development and maintenance	1,684	-	598	-	-	-

As they have not yet figured out their promotional plan going forward, for now, the Garcias have decided to increase the original promotional costs by 5% each year and revise the promotional plan for the next business plan draft.

Cross-Chapter Case Activities—Part 7

1. Open the latest Business Plan Excel Template on which you are developing the financial model for the business plan.
2. Save the Excel template using a slightly new name to reflect the current date in the first part of the file name. For example, if you completed the revision on July 15, 2021, the revised file would be named **20210715 Tech World Pro Draft Business Plan.xlsx**.

3. Promotions Assumptions *on the Promotions Worksheet*:
   - Enter the relevant promotional costs in the blue input cells on the Promotions worksheet.

4. ***Review the CashFlows, IncomeStmts, and BalSheets worksheets*** to see how the changes you made to this point impacted the financial statements.

5. Check your numbers by comparing your workbook to the following file: ***Ch 7 World Tech Pro Promotions.xlsx***.

© dotshock/Shutterstock.com

Chapter 8

First Business Plan Draft: Financial Plan

Learning Objectives

After completing this chapter, you will be able to:

◆ Develop the financial plan for a comprehensive business plan draft while ensuring that all parts of the business plan are fully integrated

◆ Develop the financial part of the business plan

Overview

The Financial Plan part of a business plan (Figure 15) retells the story of the business. Whereas the business plan to this stage describes the business through writing, this section tells the same story, but through a financial lens.

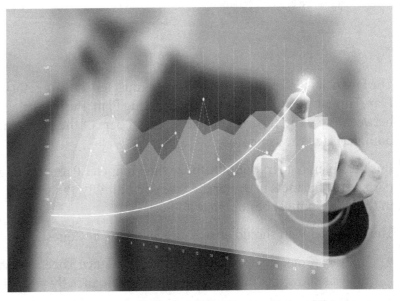

The Financial Plan includes the projected financial statements along with an investment analysis of those statements to compare the projected company financial performance against industry standards and available competitor performance. The investment analysis also includes a break-even analysis, critical success factor and sensitivity analysis, and estimated business valuation. It might also include a capitalization table showing the planned and desired percentages of ownership distributed between the founding entrepreneurs and other investors. The capitalization table should indicate the equity dilution that will occur when investors make new investments into the business during the five or more years of future operations covered by the business plan.

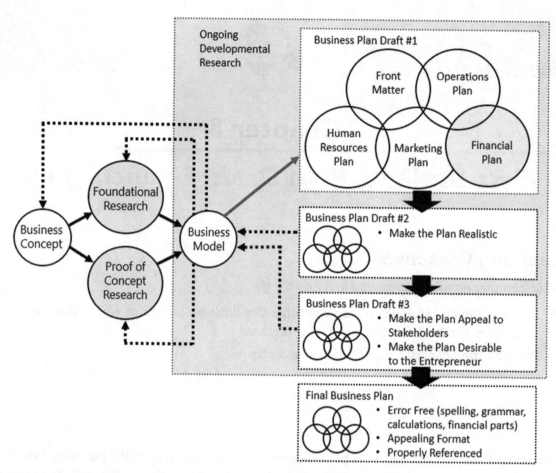

Figure 15. Financial Plan

(Illustration by Lee A. Swanson)

Financial Plan Contents

The Financial Plan part of a business plan must tell the same story as does the Front Matter, Operations Plan, Human Resources Plan, and Marketing Plan. Business plan readers expect complete consistency between the written parts and the financial part of the plan. Business plan writers must ensure that both parts tell the same story.

Business plan readers will scrutinize the Financial Plan and might study it before reading the other parts of the business plan. For the sake of credibility, the financial statements and investment analysis in this section must be complete and correct.

The Financial Plan should answer the following key questions:

- Do the projected incomes statement, balance sheets, cash flow statements, and investment analysis show that the business should be financially viable in the future?
- Do the projected statements and investment analysis tell precisely the same story as do the Front Matter, Operations Plan, Human Resources Plan, and Marketing Plan sections—one in mainly number format and the other in words?

- Is it clear what information in the projected statements is based on actual numbers and what information is based on assumptions? Are the assumptions realistic?
- What do the ratios disclose to the entrepreneur and business plan readers about the financial viability of the business?
- What is the break-even point, usually expressed in units sold and sales dollars?

Overview

Introduce a comprehensive overview that describes how the business plan writer developed the financial section. This overview should be from several paragraphs to a few pages in length and should explain the assumptions used to develop the financial model.

The overview section should also indicate that the business plan writer conducted an investment analysis and should provide an overview of the results. However, the investment analysis results from the first business plan draft are unlikely to appeal to investors or show a desirable business opportunity for the entrepreneur. So, the business plan writer should write an overview of the investment analysis results as they complete the final business plan draft. That is, after the entrepreneur adjusts the business model and strategies in the plan to make it realistic (see Chapter 9) and then further develops the business model and plan to make them appealing to investors and desirable to the entrepreneur (see Chapter 10).

Pro forma Income Statements

The business plan should include five years of projected income statements unless there is a good reason for having more or fewer years of projections.

© William Potter/Shutterstock.com

Pro forma Balance Sheets

The business plan should include five years of projected balance sheets unless there is a good reason for having more or fewer years of projections.

© William Potter/Shutterstock.com

Pro forma Cash Flow Statements

Business plan writers should prepare monthly cash flow projections for five years from business inception. By preparing the cash flow projections, the writer can estimate working capital needs and other things like the times when the business will need to draw on or can pay down loans and the months when it will need to take out longer-term loans with which to purchase fixed assets. Without a tool like this, the business plan writer will be severely handicapped when talking with bankers about the business's expected financial needs. They will want to know how large of a line of credit the business will need and when it needs to borrow longer-term money. It is only through making cash flow projections that the business plan writer will be able to answer those questions. The writer also needs that information to determine things like any needed changes to required loan payments, and when the entrepreneurs can take owner draws or pay dividends.

When using the OtherExpenses tab in the Business Plan Excel Template (Appendix C), the entrepreneur must anticipate all of the business's monthly expenses. See Appendix D for a list of the everyday expenses that appear on cash flow statements and income statements. The entrepreneur can double-check their list of expenses against those in Appendix D to see whether there are any they might need to add.

© Natee K Jindakum/Shutterstock.com

Investment Analysis

After applying the cash management approach to determine the company's financing needs (see Chapter 9), the entrepreneur can apply some financial analysis to assess the realism of the first business plan draft. The analysis will almost certainly show financial models that are unrealistic, unappealing to investors, and undesirable for the entrepreneurs. The analysis should also help the entrepreneur revise the business model and business plan draft to make them realistic when preparing the second draft (see Chapter 10). They must then conduct another round of financial analysis on the second draft results to help guide their revisions as they prepare the third and, hopefully, final draft (see Chapter 11) to make the plan appealing to investors and desirable for the entrepreneur while retaining the plan's realism.

© Freedomz/Shutterstock.com

Business plan readers will conduct analyses of their own on the projected financial statements in the final plan. Therefore, entrepreneurs must do their analyses so that they know in advance what the business plan readers will discover. If potential investors reading the plan will conclude after their analysis that the plan is either unrealistic or unappealing to them, the entrepreneur did not finish developing the plan—and should never have given it to potential investors. A sign that the entrepreneur has finished developing the plan is if potential investors evaluating its projected financial statements believe it to be realistic and appealing to them as potential investors. Of course, entrepreneurs should also ensure, through their analysis of the financial statements, that the business model and business plan is desirable to them as an owner of the new business.

So, business plan writers should perform some form of analysis on their first draft financial model to help them make the second draft realistic. They can use financial ratios and possibly a break-even analysis for this.

When the second draft of the business plan is complete, the writer should again perform ratio and break-even analyses to provide them with guidance when making the plan appealing to investors and desirable to the entrepreneur in the third and possibly final version.

After the third draft of the plan is finished, the entrepreneur's ratio and break-even analyses should show the plan to be realistic and appealing to investors, and desirable to them as the owner. If the plan does not yet meet those goals, the business plan writer must make improvements to the business and financial models until the goals are achieved. Then, the entrepreneur should have *the most likely scenario*. They can then develop *best-case* and *worst-case scenarios* using critical success factor and sensitivity analysis. After analyzing those, the entrepreneur (and investors) should have a good idea of the likely impacts on the business if the critical success factors end up being worse than expected, and better than expected. The entrepreneur should also estimate the value of the business and present a capitalization table showing the planned or proposed proportions of ownership each investor will have as they invest in the business over its first few years of operation.

Projected Financial Ratios and Industry Standard Ratios

Business plan writers should calculate the financial ratios from the projected financial statements while understanding that the ratios for the first business plan draft will likely indicate poor company performance. After analyzing the ratios, including as compared to relevant industry average ratios from sources like Stats Link Canada (2009), the entrepreneur should be prepared to revise the business model and strategies as they prepare the second draft of the business plan to be realistic.

Break-Even Analysis

Business plan writers should include a break-even analysis. The results are expressed by when the break-even point is hit (year, month), how many units of sales represent breakeven, and what dollar value of sales represents the break-even point. Breakeven can be calculated over a particular time frame using the following formulas:

- Break-even point in units = fixed costs / (price per unit − variable cost per unit)
- Break-even point in sales revenue = fixed costs / contribution margin ratio = fixed costs / ((price per unit − variable cost per unit) / price per unit)

For example, if a business's total fixed costs are $1,000,000 in a year, it costs $5.00 to produce each unit of the product, and the business sells it for $7.00 per unit, the break-even point is (1,000,000 / [7 − 5] =) 500,000 units of the product for that year.

The break-even point in sales revenue is (1,000,000 / [[7 − 5]/7]) = $3,500,000. This should be the same result as the break-even number of units multiplied by the price per unit, which was 500,000 units × $7 per unit = $3,500,000 in sales revenue.

It is rarely as easy to calculate breakeven as depicted in the previous paragraphs because many businesses have multiple product lines and other complicating factors. However, there are also other ways to calculate breakeven, including converting finished monthly cash flow statements to income statements and then seeing when the revenues begin to match expenses.

The break-even calculations can be depicted graphically and in table form, as shown in the Business Plan Excel Template (Appendix C).

Critical Success Factor and Sensitivity Analysis

The third business plan draft should be the final one if it is realistic, appealing to investors, and desirable for the entrepreneur. The financial model in the final business plan draft should be the *most likely scenario* given all the entrepreneur knows, has found out, and has confirmed through research. However, when the business plan is implemented, it is already out of date because of changes that will have occurred in its operating environment.

So, entrepreneurs should identify the factors (critical success factors) that will have negative and positive impacts on the business if the real-life outcomes turn out to be less favorable or more favorable than expected. Then, they can work from *copies* of the most likely scenario spreadsheet to prepare spreadsheets showing the *worst-case scenario* and *best-case scenario*. To do this, the business plan writer should select one or a few factors for which they have alternative projections. For example, one set of alternative projections might represent 10% lower sales revenue, which might be the likely result of a relatively severe general economic slowdown. The entrepreneur can then work from a fresh copy of the most likely scenario spreadsheet, replace the current numbers with the alternative projections, and evaluate the resulting *worst-case financial scenario.*

The second set of alternatives can represent 8% higher sales revenue, which might happen if there is a moderate general economic upswing. The writer should then use another fresh copy of the most likely scenario financial spreadsheet, input the second set of alternative numbers, and evaluate the likely outcomes from the *best-case financial scenario.*

The entrepreneur then needs to write a summary of the implications of the worst-case and best-case scenarios for the potential investors reading the plan.

Business Valuation

The third draft of the business plan should be the final one unless it is not yet entirely realistic, appealing to investors, and desirable for the entrepreneur. Then, if the entrepreneur plans to seek equity investment, they should estimate the value of the business because potential equity investors will receive an ownership interest in the company in exchange for their investment, and a valuation is required to calculate what percentage of ownership the investment will buy. For example, if the entrepreneur asks an investor for $50,000 in exchange for 30% ownership interest in the business, they are claiming that the business is worth $166,667 ($50,000 / 30%). That investor will demand to know how the entrepreneur concluded that the business was worth that much. The entrepreneur must be prepared to justify their calculations and convince the investor that $166,667 is a realistic valuation before they will accept the offer.

There are three primary business valuation methods: market, income, and cost approaches. Most valuation methods apply to businesses that have been in operation for some time and have earnings records. There are fewer methods available to entrepreneurs who have not yet started their business and whose companies have little or no earnings record.

The market approach values a company or another asset at or close to the amount at which similar companies or assets were recently sold. If a company is publicly traded, that firm's market capitalization (value) is the price per share multiplied by the number of outstanding shares. This approach can work well for assets that are frequently bought and sold, like houses. It is usually not of much use when trying to place a value on a new or young company.

The income approach is based on projected earnings while taking debt and the time value of money into account. However, it is difficult to forecast the earnings of a business, especially a new venture, and convince a potential investor that the projections are realistic. The income approach might include a multiple, meaning a figure by which the projected income will be multiplied. For example, if an entrepreneur who has projected earnings to be $100,000 over a set time determines that an appropriate multiple is 5, they would value the company at $500,000 ($100,000 × 5) in future dollars that must then be discounted to take into account the time value of money and any outstanding debt owed by the company. Many factors must be taken into account to arrive at a multiple that investors might accept.

The cost approach is a valuation technique based on the replacement cost of an asset. This approach is often used to value commercial real estate and farm businesses, especially when there have not been enough sales of similar types of properties to be able to apply the market approach. The cost approach involves estimating how much it would cost to purchase or construct similar assets, and then discounting the result to account for things like the age of the asset and how less useful or valuable it is than a new asset.

Capitalization Table

A capitalization table is not required if an entrepreneur will retain 100% ownership of their company. However, every time that other investors add money to the business in exchange for ownership, the percentages of ownership allocated to the entrepreneur and all investors will change. The capitalization table keeps a running account of the anticipated ownership changes (new equity investments or sales) and includes the dates at which each change in ownership occurs, resulting in changing ownership percentages.

The capitalization table should be linked to the investments in the company (and any ownership sales) showing on the finished version of the cash flow statement.

Chapter Summary

This chapter described the Financial Plan and explained the need to include a relatively comprehensive written overview to explain the assumptions behind, and implications from the projected income statement, balance sheet, and cash flow statements that follow the overview. The investment analysis appears after the projected financial statements. A business plan is not complete until a full investment analysis indicates that the business model and plan show a viable company backed up by realistic strategies and financial projections that are appealing to investors and desirable for the entrepreneur. The investment analysis section should include financial ratios, a break-even analysis, and a critical success factor and sensitivity analysis section that are all supported by written explanations describing what the analyses mean and their implications. If the entrepreneur plans to attract equity investors, the Financial Plan part of the business plan should include a business valuation with a full explanation of how the entrepreneur arrived at that value, and a capitalization table.

Exercises

Exercise 8.1—Write the Financial Plan

Use the Business Plan Word Template (Appendix B) to begin writing the Financial Plan.

Exercise 8.2—Develop the Financial Model Part 4

Use the Business Plan Excel Template (Appendix C) to do the following:

1. Review the schedules developed as part of Exercises 5.2, 6.2, and 7.2 and update them as needed.
2. Fill in any remaining labels and numbers in the OtherExpenses tab, using the list of common expenses from Appendix D to complete the expense list for the company.
3. Review the cash flow statements, income statements, and balance sheet to be sure that the calculations are correct.

Exercise 8.3—First Draft Financial Analyses

Use the Business Plan Excel Template (Appendix C) to do the following:

1. Look up and add the relevant industry average ratios to the RatioAnalysis tab.

2. Evaluate the ratios in the RatioAnalysis tab relative to the industry average ratios and to those of comparable companies, if available and use the analysis to plan revised strategies and financial projections to make the second draft of the business plan more realistic.

3. Review the break-even analysis on the IncomeStmts tab and use it to plan revised strategies and financial projections to make the second draft of the business plan more realistic

Cross-Chapter Case—Tech World Pro Part 8

The Initial Financial Plan

When Talia and Malik Garcia set their prices, they planned a 100% markup for all three of their retail product categories. That means that the price they planned to charge their customers would be double the cost to them of purchasing the items from their wholesalers.

Since then, the Garcias did more research and discovered that the average retail markup on the categories of computer systems, components, and supplies they plan to sell is 70%. They have decided that they must update their revenue model with the more realistic markup amount. To do this, they plan to revise their spreadsheet model to reflect a 70% markup instead of a 100% markup.

The couple has also determined that they can get a $1,500,000 mortgage to finance part of the cost of the building they plan to purchase in the amount of $2,140,000. They anticipate being able to negotiate a financing rate of 8.30% over an amortization term of 15 years (180 months). They expect that the loan terms might include an option to make an extra annual principal payment once per calendar year of up to a fixed amount, perhaps 5% of the original $1,500,000 loan amount.

Cross-Chapter Case Activities—Part 8

1. Open the latest Business Plan Excel Template on which you are developing the financial model for the business plan.

2. Save the Excel template using a slightly new name to reflect the current date in the first part of the file name. For example, if you completed the revision on August 1, 2021, the revised file would be named *20210801 Tech World Pro Draft Business Plan.xlsx*.

3. Updating assumptions *on the Retailsales Worksheet*:
   - Replace the 200% (which represents a 100% markup) previously inserted in the blue input cells in Chart 6 on the RetailSales worksheet with 170% (representing a 70% markup) for all five years.

4. Mortgage loan assumptions *on the TermLoans Worksheet*:
   - Enter the planned loan amount, number of monthly payments, and annualized interest rate amount in the blue input cells on the TermLoans worksheet.
     - Note: the TermLoans Worksheet includes a line in which additional payments can be made toward loan principal if the loan terms allow for such payments and if the company has excess cash available with which to make the extra payments.

5. *Review the CashFlows, IncomeStmts, and BalSheets worksheets* to see how the changes you made to this point impacted the financial statements.

6. Check your numbers by comparing your workbook to the following file: *Ch 8 World Tech Pro Sales update Loan.xlsx*.

© dotshock/Shutterstock.com

Chapter 9

Applying the Cash Management Approach to Determine Financing Needs

Learning Objectives

After completing this chapter, you will be able to:

◆ Describe the funding sources for start ups

◆ Apply the Cash Management Approach to determine financing needs

Overview

While chapters 4–8 outline a standard business plan structure, this chapter addresses how to apply the cash management approach to assess financing needs when planning a business (Figure 16). It also describes how to evaluate the first business plan draft—which is almost assured to be unrealistic—to guide the next phase of business plan development, converting the first draft into a realistic second business plan draft.

© PinkBlue/Shutterstock.com

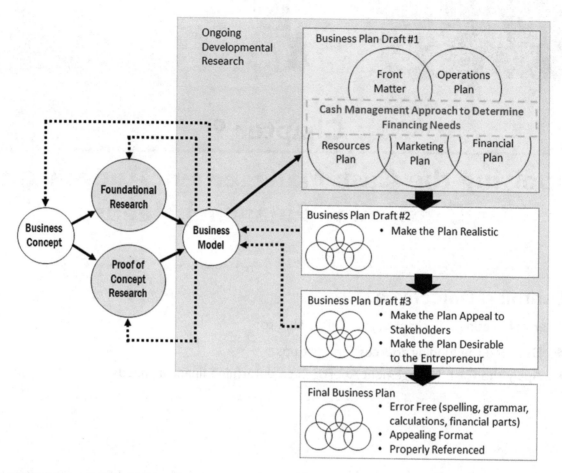

Figure 16. First Business Plan Draft

(Illustration by Lee A. Swanson)

Financing a Start Up

When financing a start up, an entrepreneur must usually use their resources along with funding from family and friends, if available. Some can access grants and prize money. When they deplete those sources, and before their business can fund itself from operations, the entrepreneur will have to seek either debt or equity financing.

Starting Capital

Entrepreneurs almost always require starting capital to move their ideas forward to the point where they can start their ventures. It is difficult to determine the amount of money needed because that requirement can change as plans evolve. Other challenges include securing the amount desired and getting it when it is needed. If an entrepreneur is unable to secure the required amount or cannot get the funding when needed, they must develop new plans.

Once a venture begins to make cash sales, or it starts to receive the money earned through credit sales, it can use those resources to fund some of its activities. Until then, it must get the money it needs through other sources.

© Den Rise/Shutterstock.com

Bootstrap financing is when entrepreneurs use their ingenuity to make their existing resources, including money and time, stretch as far as possible—usually out of necessity until they can transform their venture into one in which outside investors will want to invest.

Personal Money

Entrepreneurs will almost always have to invest personal money into their start up before they can get funding help from others. Sometimes, entrepreneurs form businesses as partnerships or as multi-owner corporations with other entrepreneurs who also personally contribute funds to the venture.

Love Money

Love money refers to funding provided by friends and family who want to support an entrepreneur, often when they have no other ready source of money after using up their available personal resources to support their start up.

Grants and Start Up Prize Money

In some cases, nonrepayable grants might be provided by governments or other agencies to support new venture start ups. Sometimes, entrepreneurs can enter business planning or similar competitions in which they might win money and other benefits, like free office or retail space or free legal or accounting services for a set period.

Debt Financing

From an entrepreneur's perspective, the cost of debt financing is the interest that they pay for the use of the money that they borrow. From an investor's perspective, their reward, or return on debt financing, is the interest that they gain in addition to the return of the money that they lent to an entrepreneur or another borrower.

The entrepreneur (borrower) must often pledge collateral to provide some protection to the investor (lender) to entice them to charge an interest rate that is low enough that it is not prohibitively costly for the borrower. If a borrower defaults on a loan, the lender can gain ownership of the property pledged as collateral. A key objective for an entrepreneur seeking debt financing is to provide sufficient collateral to get the loan but to not pledge so much that they put essential property at risk.

When entrepreneurs borrow money, they must pay it back subject to the terms of the loan. The loan terms include the specific interest rate charged and the period within which the loan needs to be repaid. There are several other loan terms and features that lenders might offer to borrowers. One such feature is whether the loan can be converted to equity at a particular point in time and according to certain criteria and subject to specific terms.

© William Potter/Shutterstock.com

Term Loans

Borrowers typically acquire term loans through a financial institution. In exchange for a particular amount of money, the borrower agrees to repay the loan over a specified term by making regular, usually monthly payments. Those payments are of a fixed amount and are blended, meaning they cover the interest owed since the last payment plus some of the principal amount of the loan. The interest rate might be fixed (fixed interest rate), or it might float (variable interest rate) as market conditions change. The loan terms offered by the financial institution are based on factors like the borrower's credit rating and whether the borrower has assets to pledge as security for the loan.

Operating Loans (Lines of Credit)

Operating loans are short-term loans businesses use when they temporarily need funds. They are prearranged up to a certain amount of money, and the borrower can automatically enact the loan and get immediate cash without making any arrangements with the financial institution beyond those that were put into place when the operating loan was set up. Operating loan interest rates, maximum loan amounts, and other terms depend on things like credit ratings and the assets the borrower pledges as security. Borrowers are usually required to make regular payments on their outstanding operating loans but might be allowed to pay the interest owned without also being required to pay part of the principal amount owed in a particular period.

Trade Credit

Sometimes, debt financing can be in the form of trade credit, where a supplier provides the product to a business but does not require payment for a specific length of time, or perhaps until the company has sold the product to a customer. Customer advances are another form of debt financing and involve a customer paying in advance for a product or service so that the business has those funds available to use to pay its suppliers.

Advantages of Debt Financing

One advantage of debt financing is that the entrepreneur does not sacrifice ownership and lose some control of their venture when they take out a loan.

Another advantage of debt financing is the certainty of the payments the borrower needs to make during the term of the loan. For example, a borrower might take out a loan for $20,000 over a five-year term at a fixed interest rate of 6.2% with a monthly payment schedule designed to pay off the entire loan by the end of its five-year term. That borrower will pay $389 per month and will owe nothing more after the five-year term. They will have paid back the entire $20,000 loan amount plus a total of $3,340 in interest.

Another advantage of debt financing is that it allows companies to *trade on equity*. Trading on equity enhances the rate of return on common shareholders' equity by using debt to finance asset purchases or to take other measures that are expected to generate more earning than the cost to service the loan. For example, if a company borrows $20,000 at 6.2% interest and uses that money to purchase a machine it will use to increase its return on equity by 20%, then it is *trading on equity* and financially better off than it would be if it had not taken out the loan. Of course, the inherent risk involved with this strategy is lowered when income streams are relatively stable.

Disadvantages of Debt Financing

When borrowing money, an entrepreneur might feel that their lenders put their interests ahead of those of the borrower. For example, some bankers might seem to have interests that do not fully align with those of the borrower. They want assurances that their bank will get all of the money back that they lent, plus all of the interest owed to them during the term of the loan. However, even though it might improve the chances that the entrepreneur can repay all of the owed money, they might not be willing—or able—to allow an entrepreneur to defer payments in months when they struggle to generate the cash flow necessary to make the loan payment.

Another disadvantage of borrowing is that the entrepreneur places their ownership of the property pledged as collateral for the loan at risk. For many new ventures, a loan is only possible to acquire if the owner provides their personal *guarantee* that the money will be paid back as outlined in the loan agreement, thus putting personal property at risk.

The further disadvantage of debt financing for start up entrepreneurs is that there are a limited number of lenders who are interested and able to provide loans to businesses during their early stages.

Equity Financing

From an entrepreneur's perspective, the cost of equity financing is the loss of some control over their venture as they must share ownership of the business. From an investor's perspective, their reward for purchasing an ownership interest in the business is the potential to share in the business's anticipated future success. They might receive this reward through dividends (a portion of the profit distributed to owners) and by being able to sell their ownership interest to another investor  (or back to the entrepreneur) for more than the amount they spent when purchasing the ownership interest.

The protection for the investor if they are a *shareholder* is in the influence they might be able to exert in the company's decision-making processes. This influence is ordinarily proportionate to their share of the ownership in the overall business. Equity investors typically seek to earn a competitive return on their investment that is in line with the level of risk they assume by investing in the business. The riskier the investment, the higher the return the investor expects.

The following are some potential sources of equity financing for start up entrepreneurs:

Equity Crowdfunding

Equity crowdfunding is a relatively new way for entrepreneurs to raise capital, and it involves using online methods to promote equity interests in ventures to potential investors.

Angel Investors

Angel investors are wealthy individuals who, on their own, or with other angel investors, invest in new ventures in exchange for an ownership interest in the business. Sometimes, angels invest in companies in exchange for convertible debt, an investment that starts as a loan, usually in the form of a bond, that they have the option to convert to an equity interest in the company at a particular point in time for a predetermined number of shares. Angel investors are generally less restricted in what kinds of investments they will consider than are venture capitalists, who often invest other people's pooled money. Like venture capitalists, however, angel investors usually undertake a rigorous *due diligence* process to determine whether to invest in the opportunities they are considering.

Venture Capital

Venture capital is raised when investors pool their money. The venture capital company then very carefully invests the money in the fund in existing companies that are expected to experience high growth. The venture capital company does not expect to invest for long, and it expects to generate a substantial return. For example, it might expect to invest in an opportunity for a period of up to five years and then get out of the investment with five times the money it originally invested. Of course, only some investment opportunities will generate the returns hoped for, and others will return far less than expected.

Venture capitalists might exert some ownership control by influencing some business decisions in cases where they believe that by doing so, they can protect their investment or cause the investment to produce higher returns. However, they generally prefer to invest in companies that are going to be well run and will not require them to be involved in making operational decisions for the company. Venture capitalists might also provide some assistance, such as business advice, to the companies in which they invest.

A *venture round* refers to a phase of financing that institutional investors like venture capitalists provide to entrepreneurs. The first phase (sometimes following a *seed round* in which entrepreneurs themselves provide the start up capital and then an *angel round* where angel investors invest in the company) is called *Series A*. Subsequent venture rounds are indicated by letters, like *Series B* and *Series C*.

In general, because venture capitalists typically invest investors' money, they are obligated to assume a limited amount of risk and usually do not invest in start up companies.

Due Diligence

Investors follow due diligence processes to assess the risk and potential return associated with the investments they are considering. As such, entrepreneurs should maintain a due diligence file that they can provide to desirable potential investors who express an interest in their venture.

A due diligence file will include copies of many of the legal papers and other essential documents that a venture has accumulated and that tells the story of the enterprise. These documents will include those related to incorporation, securities it has issued or is in the process of issuing, loans, contracts, intellectual property documents, tax information, financial statements, and other documentation.

Advantages of Equity Financing

A benefit to equity financing is that it does not usually require a regular payback from cash flow.

Unlike with debt financing, equity investments do not usually give rise to a regular encumbrance that can increase the difficulty a young company might have in meeting its regular monthly expenses.

Second, when a firm uses equity financing, it does not need to pledge collateral, which means that the company does not place its assets at risk.

Another advantage with equity financing is that, depending on the form of financing and who the investors are, a firm might gain valued advisers. Also, investors who exercise their ownership rights to have a say in the operations of the company, or who otherwise provide advice and mentorship to entrepreneurs starting ventures, are usually highly motivated to help the company succeed. Investors expect to benefit only when the companies they invest in succeed, meaning that their financing incentives are aligned with those of the entrepreneur and other owners.

Disadvantages of Equity Financing

It is often more challenging to raise equity financing than debt financing. Second, when they share ownership in exchange for investment into their business, entrepreneurs give up a portion of the value that they create. If things do not go as planned, entrepreneurs can lose control of their companies to their investors.

Applying the Cash Management Approach to Determining Financing Needs

Cash management is one of the most critical functions an entrepreneur must perform when preparing a business plan. Business plan writers should use the cash management principles and the approach described in this section to help determine how much financing the business needs and precisely when it needs it.

The cash management approach to determining financing needs begins with the premise that all projected month-end cash balances must be positive and should fall within a specified range. The planning required to ensure that the desired month-end cash balances fall within the range also serves to help business planners figure out the company's financing requirements.

© Andrii Yalanskyi/Shutterstock.com

If a projected month-end cash balance falls below the target range, the entrepreneur must revise their plan to increase the amount of available cash to pay for their planned purchases and activities or decrease their cash requirements.

Entrepreneurs have the following methods available to increase the projected amounts of money when needed:

- An entrepreneur might infuse an equity investment into their company, either by investing more of their own money or finding a willing external investor.

- They might be able to secure a term loan they can pay back over an extended period.

- Many entrepreneurs can acquire operating loans to bridge shorter periods between when they need the money and expect to have it.

- Entrepreneurs might be able to implement measures to increase revenues or revise their existing projections based on realistic assumptions.

- Some businesses that generate excess cash in busy months save it to use in months when they expect to make fewer sales.

- In some cases, a business might be able to generate needed cash by selling an asset they no longer need.

Alternatively, if one or more months show projected cash amounts below that desired, the entrepreneur can apply one or more of the following methods to decrease the expected need for money:

- A business can often realistically reduce planned expenditures by cutting costs or eliminating, deferring, or reducing planned purchases of inventory and other assets.

- An overall strategy to reduce projected expenditures is to consider ways to reduce ongoing human resources, facility rental, and raw materials or merchandise inventory costs. These strategies might include ways to conduct business with fewer employees or different compensation strategies, including incentive-based pay systems or bonus pay based on performance. Sometimes, a company can start operations in a small facility and later move to a larger one, or an entrepreneur might be able to initially work out of a home office or coworking space before moving to a dedicated facility. Depending on what the product strategy is, an entrepreneur might be able to find more cost-effective suppliers.

If a projected ending cash balance is higher than the planned range, and if the projections are realistic and don't overstate likely cash inflows or understate cash outflows, the entrepreneur must revise their plan to use the excess cash productively. The entrepreneur can take one or more of the following actions:

- If future month projections show a shortage of cash, the entrepreneur can move the excess money to temporary savings for later use.
- If allowed according to the loan terms, the entrepreneur can use the excess cash to pay off or reduce the loan principal owed.
- The entrepreneur can pay dividends to the owners, including themselves. Some business owners use dividends to pay themselves instead of drawing a salary from their business operations.
- In some cases, excess cash from company operations might be used to buy back ownership from shareholders.
- Another use for excess cash that won't be needed within a short while, is to invest it back in the business to improve future profitability by purchasing more space, new equipment, hiring extra workers, purchasing raw materials or merchandise inventory before prices increase (and if storage space is available), or using the money in other ways that improve the future outlook for the company.

To implement the cash management approach to determining financing needs, entrepreneurs should use the following process:

1. The entrepreneur should complete the first draft of the business plan, including a full financial model populated with all the needed numbers, even if doing so requires using estimates that the entrepreneur will later replace with accurate figures.

2. Then, the entrepreneur should choose a target range in which all end-of-month cash balances should fall.

   The minimum number in the target range must always be above zero because the business cannot spend more cash in a month than it has available. It should also be at a level that protects the entrepreneur from being short of cash in a month when there are unplanned expenses because of an emergency or other occurrences.

   The maximum number in the target range should not be so high that the entrepreneur risks having too much idle cash when it could be put to a better use, like paying down debt.

   The spread between the minimum and maximum numbers could be relatively narrow, but it is easier to manage the cash amounts if the spread is at least a thousand dollars or more. For example, an entrepreneur developing a business plan for a small clothing retail store might want to have a minimum cash balance of $5,000 at the end of every month because that is the amount an emergency order would cost if the business needs additional stock. It might also be the minimum balance required by the bank for them to waive the monthly service charge.

The entrepreneur might decide that it is reasonable to have a maximum balance of up to $8,000 because they do not believe that the business would need more than that to cover any unforeseen emergency in a month.

3. The business plan writer should then add the owners' cash investments to the financial model.

4. Any predetermined initial loan amounts the entrepreneur expects to secure should be added.

5. Finally, the entrepreneur should, in turn, examine each month's ending balance on the cash flow statements, starting with the first month and ending with the last month in the financial model, usually the 12th month of the fifth year. Whenever an ending cash balance falls outside the target range, they must adapt the financial model to ensure the monthly balance falls within the target range. If they are not already confident in their revenue and expense projections, they should start by revising those. If they are satisfied with their revenue and expense projections, they must take one or more of the actions described in this chapter to make sure that the month-end cash balances fall within the predetermined range.

This step can be time consuming, but it is an efficient way for the entrepreneur to determine their financing requirements while also improving their strategies for running the company.

6. After completing the previous step and confirming that all end-of-month closing cash balances are positive and fall within the target range, the entrepreneur should turn their attention to making their business plan more realistic. Making it more realistic involves evaluating the amount and types of financing revealed when applying the cash management approach to determining the required funding. The entrepreneur must assess the likelihood of getting the needed financial support when and in the amounts necessary.

7. When assessing the draft plan's realism, the entrepreneurs should also apply tools like breakeven and ratio analysis. Analyses of the draft financial projections might show that it will take an unrealistic (or an undesirable) amount of time for the company to breakeven and that the financial ratios reveal a poor projected financial performance when compared against industry standards and, if available, similar companies in the same industry.

The entrepreneur should use their analysis of the draft financial projections to develop a realistic second draft of their business plan. As described in Chapter 10, they should then redo the work they did in steps five to seven abovementioned and confirm that the revised plan is realistic.

Chapter Summary

This chapter described the financing options for start ups. It then described how to apply the cash management approach to determine the company's financing needs. Then, some financial analysis is required to guide the development of the second, and more realistic business plan draft.

Exercises

Exercise 9.1—Cash Management Approach

Apply the cash management approach described in this chapter, to determine the financing requirements for the business plan you are writing and to help you assess how to improve its realism.

Cross-Chapter Case—Tech World Pro Part 9

Applying the Cash Management Approach

Based on their risk assessments regarding appropriate amounts of liquid cash to have available on-hand at the end of each month considering their projected payroll obligations and market risks, and while anticipating some inflation in years 3 to 5, Talia and Malik Garcia decided that Tech World Pro should maintain the following minimum and maximum ending cash balances.

- Year 1—minimum $8,000 and maximum $15,000
- Year 2—minimum $8,000 and maximum $15,000
- Year 3—minimum $8,500 and maximum $15,500
- Year 4—minimum $9,000 and maximum $16,000
- Year 5—minimum $9,500 and maximum $16,500

Talia and Malik planned to invest their savings of $50,000 in their company at start up in January 2022.

The couple was not sure how much money their parents and Talia's aunt might be willing to invest in the business or what kind of return they might seek. However, to determine their financing needs (for the first draft of their business plan), the Garcias planned to enter the required financing amounts and worry later about who they would ask for financial assistance.

The Garcias knew they would eventually have to sit down with their parents and Talia's aunt to confirm whether they would be willing to invest in the company, and under what terms. The couple was uneasy about the idea of asking family members to invest in their business unless they believed that they could return the invested money with a reasonable return—although perhaps not at the same rate of return demanded by angel investors and venture capitalists (multiples of the amount they invested, and a relatively short investment period of only a few years). In a recent discussion, Talia and Malik shared their mutual unease about the thought of relying too much on family members to help finance their start up.

Cross-Chapter Case Activities—Part 9

1. Open the latest Business Plan Excel Template on which you are developing the financial model for the business plan.
2. Save the Excel template using a slightly new name to reflect the current date in the first part of the file name. For example, if you completed the revision on August 10, 2021, the revised file would be named **20210810 Tech World Pro Draft Business Plan.xlsx**.
3. Enter the desired month-end cash balance ranges **on the CashFlows Worksheet**:
   - Enter the desired minimum and maximum end-of-month cash balances for each year in the charts labeled "Month-End Cash Balance Target Range" located immediately below the cash flow statements.

4. Enter the owners' initial equity investment **on the CashFlows Worksheet**:

   - On the chart labeled "Equity Investments, Dividends, and Buybacks" below the cash flow statements, enter the planned initial equity investment in the January 2022 blue input cell.

5. Apply the cash management approach to determining financing needs **on the CashFlows Worksheet**:

   - If the amount showing in the first month "Cash at Month End" cell is highlighted in a red color, the amount falls outside the target end-of-month cash target range. Take action to make the number in the cell fall within the range. Once in range, the number will appear in black.

     o If the number is below the month-end cash balance target range, enter a number in the "Equity Investments by Owners" line for that month to make the cash at month end for that month fall within the target range on the cash flow statement.

     o If the number is above the month-end cash balance target range, enter a number in the "Additions from Cash" line for that month in the "Internal Investment Account" chart to make the cash at month end fall within the target range on the cash flow statement.

   - Find the next cash at month end amount on the cash flow statement that is showing in red. Note whether the number in that cell is higher or lower than the month-end cash balance target range for that month.

     o If the number is below the month-end cash balance target range *and if there is available cash in the Internal Investment Account*, enter a number in the "Cash out for Operations" line (up to the amount available in that account) to make the cash at month end for that month fall within the target range on the cash flow statement. If there is insufficient cash available in the Internal Investment Account, make up the difference by entering a number in the "Equity Investments by Owners" line for that month that will make the cash at month end for that month fall within the target range on the cash flow statement

     o If the number is above the month-end cash balance target range, enter a number in the "Additions from Cash" line for that month in the "Internal Investment Account" chart to make the cash at month end for that month fall within the target range on the cash flow statement.

   - Repeat the earlier step as you move from left to right until all the cash at month-end amounts for all five years fall within the desired month-end cash balance target ranges. However, if the cash at month-end amounts in the cash flow statement appear to be consistently higher than the desired end-of-month target range, rather than use the Internal Investment Account, you might be able to use the excess cash to pay dividends to the owners by using the "Dividend Payments to Owners" row. Note that, rather than paying dividends, you could use the "Equity Buyback from Investors" line on the chart to buy back some of the ownership interest from investors. However, if you buy back equity from investors, you must keep track of the amounts individual investors have invested, and avoid buying back more than they own.

   - After you finish making sure that the end-of-month cash balances fall within the required ranges for all five years, you can assess whether the cash projections indicate that dividends can be paid. To do so, consider the lowest closing balance in the Internal Investment Account in each year. If desired and possible, pay that amount or something less than that in dividends by registering your chosen amount somewhere in the Dividend Payments chart. When you do so, you need to also readjust the amounts *for that month* in the Internal Investment Account.

6. ***Review the CashFlows, IncomeStmts, and BalSheets worksheets*** to see how the changes you made to this point impacted the financial statements.

7. Check your numbers by comparing your workbook to the following file: ***Ch 9 World Tech Pro Cash Management.xlsx***. Note that your numbers are unlikely to match those in the noted file as you likely used different equity, internal investment account, and dividend payment numbers to make the cash at month-end amounts for all five years fall within the desired month-end cash balance target ranges.

© dotshock/Shutterstock.com

Chapter 10

Second Business Plan Draft: Making the Business Plan Realistic

Learning Objectives

After completing this chapter, you will be able to:

◆ Develop the second draft of the business plan by applying revision methods to improve the realism of the first draft

Overview

The first draft of a business plan will inevitably be unrealistic for a host of reasons. It is likely to include contradictions and gaps in the written sections, the financial and written parts might not align with each other, and sales and cash flow projections might be unrealistic. Revised strategies and projections will undoubtedly be required to convert the first draft of the business plan into a *realistic* second draft (see Figure 17).

© Blue Planet Studio/Shutterstock.com

The entrepreneur must continually improve assumptions and replace as many of them as possible with factual information to improve the realism of a draft business plan. They must then apply cash management methods, including increasing revenues or reducing expenses or planning to acquire financing in months when there is insufficient available cash. This chapter expands on the cash management approach introduced in Chapter 9 to help business plan writers convert the first business plan draft into a more realistic second draft.

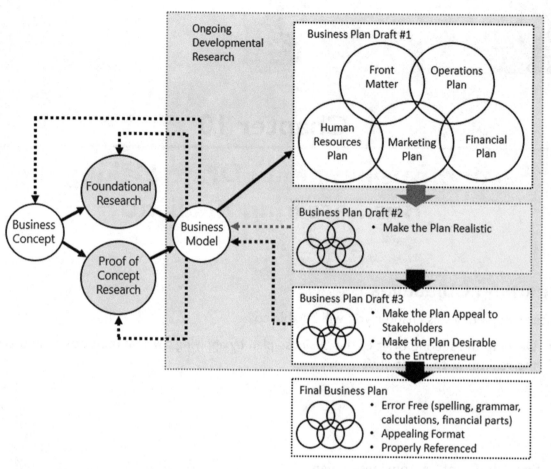

Figure 17.   Making the Business Plan Realistic

(Illustration by Lee A. Swanson)

Revising the First Business Plan Draft

Potential investors demand compelling evidence before they will believe what entrepreneurs presented in a business plan. They require proof that the entrepreneur used factual information backed up by valid research or acknowledged personal expertise, and made realistic assumptions when a claim could not be proven to be true.

Entrepreneurs necessarily base their first business plan draft on many assumptions and on plans and strategies that they had yet to test. They should replace as many of those assumptions as possible with factual and real

information when they develop the second draft of the plan. Also, first drafts often do not yet include realistic financing plans, because it is only by developing a first draft that the entrepreneur has the preliminary business model and a set of strategies available from which to determine financing needs as part of developing the second draft. So, when updating the first draft of the business plan to a more realistic second draft, apply the following process:

1. Revise the revenue and general expense projections to make them more realistic.

   Do this by replacing assumed numbers with real company data or better assumptions. Real company numbers, or industry norms, might be available from published sources or from industry professionals who might be able to provide that information to the entrepreneur.

   As shown in Figure 17, if the entrepreneur cannot realistically revise the revenue and expense projections, they might need to revisit and revise the business model. If the business model requires substantial changes, the entrepreneur might need to generate another first business plan draft before restarting this process to convert it into a realistic second draft.

2. Adjust human resources, contractor, promotions, and other costs to align with the revised projected revenues.

3. Replace assumed asset, construction, and other costs with real prices and quotes.

4. Repeat the cash management exercise to determine financing needs (see Chapter 9). Note that, before doing this, it is often easier to first delete the numbers used when completing the previous cash management approach.

5. Evaluate the new financial model using breakeven and ratio analysis. If necessary, repeat steps one to five until the financial statements are realistic.

6. Synchronize the written and financial parts of the plan. Depending on how much the entrepreneur changed the business model, revenue and expense projections, and the other costs and strategies, they might need to rewrite parts of the front matter and operations, human resources, and marketing plans—and possibly the written introduction to the financial plan. The business plan writer must ensure that the written part of the business plan tells the same story as does the financial part.

Chapter Summary

This chapter described the process for converting a copy of the first draft of the business plan into a realistic second draft.

Exercises

Exercise 10.1—Making the Business Plan Realistic

Evaluate your business plan draft and develop strategies to make it more realistic. Consider revising the revenue and general expense projections to make them more realistic. If needed, revisit and revise the business model. As needed, adjust human resource, contractor, promotions, and other costs to align them with any revised projected revenues, and replace assumed asset, construction, and other costs with real prices or quotes.

Synchronize the written and financial parts of the plan.

Cross-Chapter Case—Tech World Pro Part 10

Making the Business Plan Realistic

When reviewing their projected income statement (see the file named *Ch 9 World Tech Pro Cash Management.xlsx*), Talia and Malik Garcia noticed that the first three years showed a net loss, meaning the break-even point was sometime in the fourth year of operations.

To confirm this, they considered their break-even analysis (in units and sales dollars) for the retail sales part of their business shown in the two sets of calculations beside the income statement. Note that the break-even calculations were only based on the projected retails sales as the couple's projected service sales were relatively unsubstantial.

From the calculations, Talia and Malik saw that it was only in year 5 when their projections showed enough retail units and sales dollars to exceed the break-even units and sales amounts. The reason these calculations showed the breakeven in year 5 instead of year 4 was because the calculations did not include the planned service sales, only the projected retails sales.

The Garcias were not pleased with the idea that their business was not projected to breakeven until year 5, so they considered the following actions to improve their break-even point:

- They could find lower cost suppliers for their computer systems, components, and supplies. They could also increase prices. Either of those actions (or a combination of both) would increase the company's margins and shorten the length of time it would take to breakeven. One of the last adjustments the Garcias made to their plan was to drop their expected markup from 100% to 70%. They would prefer a higher markup, which they might achieve with a lower cost supplier.

- Talia and Malik might also seek to increase their service sales relative to the retail sales as the service sales margin would be quite high if they could keep their service people busy.

- The couple might also be able to lower their expenses. They noticed that their facility costs included property taxes of between $6,523 in year 1 and $7,342 in year 5 and loan interest exceeded $100,000 per year in each of the five years. They also budgeted over $1,000 each year for property maintenance, which they felt might be too low. They wondered what the impact on their projected financial situation would be if they lowered their debt by renting instead of purchasing land and a building.

The Garcias looked up industry average ratios from a large national database provided by the national government. They downloaded a report using the appropriate North American Industry Classification System (NAICS) code (NAICS 443144—Computer and software stores) and added the information in the blue cells on the RatioAnalysis tab. They then calculated the numbers in the green-colored cells to show their company financial projections beside some of the relevant industry numbers.

Based on the projected financial statement ratio comparisons with the industry average ratios, the couple was considering the following.

- They felt that perhaps they needed more inventory. The industry average current asset and merchandise inventory amounts seemed to indicate that computer stores generally held more inventory than they had planned to purchase for their store.

- They wondered if they could purchase some of their inventory on credit because the industry average current liabilities amounts seemed to indicate that their competitors might have access to more trade credit than they were expecting to be able to get.

- They noticed that the industry average accounts receivable amounts indicated that some of their competitors might be making more credit sales than they had planned to make. They decided to look into whether they were planning to sell too large of a proportion of their retail products to general consumers and not enough to commercial customers—who would probably demand that the Garcias offer them credit terms. Of course, this would require them to do more market research, including learning about the benefits of targeting more of the commercial market.

Talia and Malik looked at the schedules below their cash flow statements that they used to manage their cash at month-end amounts; they saw a fairly regular pattern.

In August and September, and again in November and December, they expected to generate sufficient cash inflows through sales to cover all the expenses in those months. However, during the remaining eight months of the year (January to July and October) their projections showed that their business would operate with an operating deficit where cash inflows from sales were less than monthly expenses. In those eight months, they required cash infusions from investments or accumulated savings to be able to meet all of their financial commitments.

When reviewing the projected balance sheet and cash flow statements, the Garcias saw that—in order to have enough cash on hand to make up for monthly operational cash shortfalls—they needed to keep more cash in their Internal Investment Account than was realistic for a start up.

Based on the above, Talia and Malik were considering the following.

- They were determined to smoothen out their sales patterns to become less reliant on the consumer back-to-school and Christmas seasons. By shifting their sales emphasis to commercial customers and by selling a greater proportion of service versus retail sales in their overall sales numbers, they felt that they could reduce the number of months when they would have operational cash shortfalls.
- They were again wondering whether they could increase margins on retail sales and perhaps reduce costs by renting a property instead of buying one.

Besides their $50,000, the couple's financial model included the $1,500,000 mortgage on their store property purchase and an infusion of $1,215,000 of family money, all in year 1. According to their projections, they had the cash available to pay $50,000 in dividends in year 4 and another $40,000 in year 5 (see the file named ***Ch 9 World Tech Pro Cash Management.xlsx***).

Although their current financial model showed that they had access to sufficient capital through family to start their business, Talia and Malik were uneasy with the prospect of using such large family investments to start their business—especially when they were not forecasting any payback of that money besides the potential to return the two nominal dividend amounts to their family investors.

The Garcias wondered what the situation would look like if they were to drop the idea of purchasing a property and rent a facility instead. They expected that would significantly reduce their need for family money and for such a large start up loan. Their start up loan was to be secured by the property, but they felt they could instead get a start up loan backed by family members who would cosign the loan papers to guarantee payment if they were unable to meet the loan payment commitments. Talia and Malik felt more at ease with that approach.

After conducting further research, and based on the lessons learned from their review of the first financial model draft, the Garcias decided to do the following:

- They planned to clear the loan and cash management approach from the model so they could perform a fresh cash management exercise to determine their financing needs after implementing the following changes to their financial model.
- They planned to clear the land and building purchase amounts from the asset purchases part of their financial model and clear the property tax and property maintenance amounts from the expenses.

- They estimated that they could lease a 3,500-square foot space at a net lease rate of $24.00 per square foot with occupancy costs of $3.67 per square foot for the first three years after which the annual cost would increase by 3%. This would mean that their monthly leasing costs for the first three years would be $8,070 (= 3,500 × [$24.00 + $3.67] / 12 months). The couple felt that they could negotiate a two-month free rent period for set up.

- The Garcias estimated that they would likely still need to spend about $60 per square foot to *build out* their retail space for a total renovation cost of $210,000 (= 3,500 × $60), including the cost of internal and external signage, electricity upgrades, installing shelving, and making their store appealing to customers. Additionally, an accountant friend told the couple that only about $50,000 of that amount might be depreciable.

- After talking to experts and evaluating the commercial market, Talia and Malik felt that there was an opportunity to fill a market need for computer equipment for commercial customers. This would smoothen out their seasonality estimates as follows:

  o Year 1: Jan–Feb, 0%; Mar–May, 8.9%; June–July, 8.4%; Aug–Sept, 10.4%; Oct, 8.9%; Nov–Dec, 13.4%

  o Years 2–5: Jan–Feb, 7%; Mar–May, 7.5%; June–July, 7%; Aug–Sept, 9%; Oct, 7.5%; Nov–Dec, 12%

- The Garcias also learned that, especially when selling to commercial customers, their plan to stock initial inventory equaling their projected sales for the first four months (27 systems computer systems, 728 components, and 2,154 units of computer supplies) would be inadequate, and would also fail to make their store look fully stocked on and after their opening day. So, they decided to order initial inventory amounts for all three of their product categories equal to their first seven months of projected sales.

- In preliminary discussions with potential suppliers, the couple believed that their projected unit costs are about right, but that they should be able to negotiate credit terms with their vendors resulting in the following percentage of their purchases for which they would have to pay cash.

	Year 1	Year 2	Year 3	Year 4	Year 5
Computer systems	80%	80	60	40	40
Computer components	80%	80	75	60	60
Computer supplies	100%	100	100	100	100

- The Garcias believed that by shifting their emphasis to commercial sales, they would sell more computer systems and computer components, but that their projected markup amounts would stay the same.

  o Their revised projected sales in units are as follows:

	Year 1	Year 2	Year 3	Year 4	Year 5
Computer systems	175	220	275	350	450
Computer components	4,150	5,000	6,000	6,800	7,500
Computer supplies	13,500	15,800	19,800	22,600	24,500

- They decided to ask their family members to cosign a loan so that they could borrow $150,000 at a rate of 8.3% over a 10-year (120 months) term to finance their initial inventory. They would also invest their own $50,000 and seek additional cash investments from family members if and when needed. The Garcias were anxious to find out if their financial projections would be sufficient to be able to pay dividends to their investors (including themselves) plus allow them to buy back some or all of the equity investments made by their family members as they wanted to eventually become the sole owners of their business.

- At this time, the couple hoped that they would not have to extend credit to their customers, but they realized that they might have to do so at some point.

Cross-Chapter Case Activities—Part 10

1. Open the latest Business Plan Excel Template on which you are developing the financial model for the business plan.

2. Save the Excel template using a slightly new name to reflect the current date in the first part of the file name. For example, if you completed the revision on August 15, 2021, the revised file would be named *20210815 Tech World Pro Draft Business Plan.xlsx*.

3. Reset the loan amount from $1,500,000 to zero in the blue cell *on the TermLoans Worksheet*.

4. Reset the numbers in the Equity Investments, Dividends, and Buybacks schedule to zero in the blue input cells for years 1 to 5 *on the CashFlows Worksheet*.

5. Reset the numbers in the Internal Investment Account schedule to zero in the blue input cells for years 1 to 5 *on the CashFlows Worksheet*.

6. Reset the land and building purchase amounts to zero (from $122,000 and $2,140,000) in the blue cells *on the AssetPurchases Worksheet*.

7. Change the renovations amount from $225,000 to $50,000 *on the AssetPurchases Worksheet*.

8. Add an entry titled "Undepreciable renovation costs" and add the portion of the renovation costs that are undepreciable, $160,000 (= $210,000–50,000) *on the Set Up Worksheet*.

9. Reset the Property Taxes and Property Maintenance amounts to zero in the blue cells for years 1 to 5 *on the OtherExpenses Worksheet*.

10. Add the monthly lease amount *on the OtherExpenses Worksheet*.
    - Input zero for the first two months of year 1 and add $8,070 to the remaining months
    - Change the first two cells on that line for year 2 to blue input cells, and insert $8,070
    - Change the inflation factor to zero for years 2 and 3 and to 3% for years 4 and 5

11. Do the following *on the RetailSales Worksheet*.
    - Reset the monthly seasonality percentages for all five years to match the new estimates.
    - Reset the Projected Sales in Units values for years 1 to 5.
    - Reset the initial inventory amounts to match the new plan (equal to the first seven months of projected sales).
    - Reset the Terms Extended by Vendors percentages for years 1 to 5.

12. Enter the planned loan amount, number of monthly payments, and annualized interest rate amount in the blue input cells *on the TermLoans Worksheet*.

13. Use the Cash Management Approach *on the CashFlows Worksheet*.
    - Use the same desired minimum and maximum end of month cash balances targets as before.
    - Remember to add the Garcia's $50,000 equity investment in the first month along with additional equity investments as required to provide the ending cash balance amounts desired.
    - Use the Equity Envestments, Dividends, and Buybacks schedule and the Internal Investment Account schedule to complete the cash management approach exercise to make sure that all month-end cash balances fall within the target ranges.

14. *Review the CashFlows, IncomeStmts, and BalSheets worksheets* to see how the changes you made to this point impacted the financial statements.

15. Check your numbers by comparing your workbook to the following file: *Ch 10 World Tech Pro Making it More Real.xlsx*. Note that your numbers are unlikely to match those in the noted file as you likely used different equity, internal investment account, and dividend payment numbers to make the cash at month-end amounts for all five years fall within the desired month-end cash balance target ranges.

© dotshock/Shutterstock.com

Chapter 11

Third Business Plan Draft: Making the Plan Appeal to Stakeholders and Desirable to the Entrepreneur

Learning Objectives

After completing this chapter, you will be able to:

◆ Develop the third draft of the business plan by applying revision methods to improve the realism of the second draft while also making it desirable to the entrepreneur and appealing to targeted investors

Overview

This chapter deals with adjusting the second business plan draft to retain, and possibly improve, its realism, while also making it appealing to targeted investors and desirable to the entrepreneur (Figure 18). In some cases, a business plan should also be made to appeal to other targeted stakeholders, such as highly skilled but difficult to recruit employees who need assurance of the venture's potential or a minority ownership offer before considering a job offer.

© Roman Samborskyi/Shutterstock.com

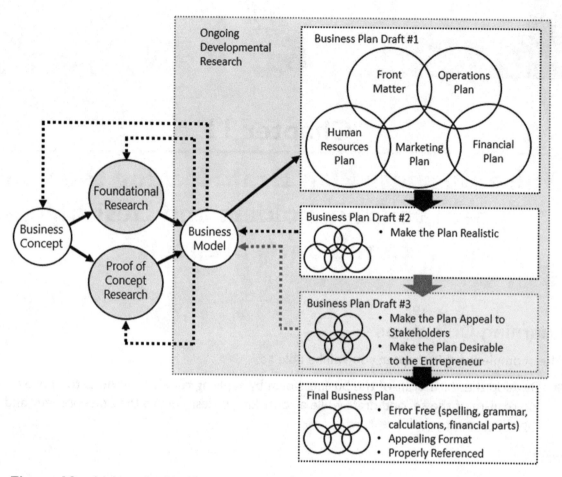

Figure 18.   Making the Plan Appeal to Stakeholders and Desirable to the Entrepreneur

(Illustration by Lee A. Swanson)

How to Make the Plan Appealing and Desirable

As shown in Figure 18, the goal of the third draft of the business plan is to, while retaining the realism, make the plan appealing to stakeholders and desirable to the entrepreneur.

A business plan that has realistic strategies and financial projections does not necessarily describe a venture that meets investor needs or provides enough benefit to the entrepreneur to warrant implementing the plan. Usually, the business plan writer needs to convert a realistic second business plan draft into a third draft with revised strategies and projections, making it appealing to investors and worthwhile for the entrepreneur to implement.

The process for converting a realistic second business plan draft into an appealing and desirable third and final draft is similar to the cash management process described in Chapter 9, but with further analysis to determine what is required to meet investor and entrepreneur needs. The steps for making a plan appealing and desirable are as follows:

1. Based on the tentative financing methods established in the second business plan draft, determine what targeted investors require from the business to invest in it.

2. The entrepreneur should determine in concrete terms what they desire from the business.

   An entrepreneur is more likely to achieve the personal goals they want from their business if they immediately incorporate business strategies consistent with those goals. Examples of personal goals entrepreneurs want to achieve by operating a venture include the following:

   - Operate the business until age 65 and comfortably retire by living off the sale proceeds.
   - Develop the venture as a family business to turn over to the children when the entrepreneur turns age 60 while retaining enough ownership to retire by living off annual dividends from the business.
   - Live a good work–life balance by getting the company started and then turning over its management to trusted employees that the entrepreneur regularly monitors while limiting their involvement in day-to-day activities.
   - Set up a business to grow through hard but satisfying work into a large corporation.
   - Operate a lifestyle business, like a bed and breakfast, that gives the entrepreneur something meaningful to do while earning a modest living.

   These examples show a wide range of possible entrepreneur desires. To achieve their goals by running a business, entrepreneurs must implement the appropriate strategies.

3. Make a new copy of the second business plan draft.

4. While retaining their realism, revise the revenue and general expense projections to meet targeted investor needs and the entrepreneur's desires.

   If realistic revisions are insufficient to meet one or both of those needs and desires, as shown in Figure 18, the entrepreneur will need to revisit and revise the business model. If the required business model changes are substantial, the entrepreneur might need to effectively generate another first business plan draft to convert into a realistic second draft and third draft that is appealing and desirable.

5. Adjust human resource, contractor, promotions, and other costs to align them with revised projected revenues.

6. Replace assumed asset, construction, and other costs with real prices or quotes.

7. Delete the loans previously added to the financial model because different loan amounts and borrowing dates will be required after the abovementioned revisions to the plan.

8. Delete the values added to the Equity Investments, Internal Investment Account, and Dividend Payments schedules located below the Cash Flow statements as different values will be required after making the abovementioned revisions.

9. As necessary, revise the target range for end-of-month cash balances.

10. Add the entrepreneurs' personal investments and any other cash investments from the owners to the Equity Investments schedule.

11. Add any initial loan amounts the entrepreneur expects to secure.

12. Apply measures to make each month's ending balance on the cash flow statements fall within the target range (see Chapter 9).

13. Evaluate the revised financial model and if it is not realistic or does not indicate an appealing investment opportunity or a business that can achieve the entrepreneurs' goals, revisit and revise the business model or—if relatively minor revisions are required using the same business model—restart at step one above.

14. Synchronize the written and financial parts of the plan.

Chapter Summary

After developing the first business plan draft, an entrepreneur will inevitably need to make some significant adjustments to the business model and accompanying strategies to make it realistic. After that, the entrepreneur needs to shift their attention to maintaining and potentially further improving the realism of the plan while making it desirable to the entrepreneur and appealing to targeted investors. This chapter describes a process for converting a realistic second business plan draft into a third and final draft that meets the needs of investors and the entrepreneur.

Exercises

Exercise 11.1—Making the Business Plan Appealing to Investors and Desirable to the Entrepreneur

Convert the second business plan draft into a realistic third and final draft that is appealing to investors and can help the entrepreneur develop a business that meets their goals. Review the step-by-step process described in the "How to Make the Plan Appealing and Desirable" section of this chapter.

1. Determine what targeted investors require from the business to invest in it.

2. Describe what the entrepreneur wants from the business.

3. While retaining their realism, revise the business plan draft to meet targeted investor's needs and the entrepreneur's desires.

4. Synchronize the written and financial parts of the plan.

Cross-Chapter Case—Tech World Pro Part 11

Making the Business Plan Appealing to Stakeholders and Desirable to the Entrepreneur

Talia and Malik Garcia reviewed their new projected income statement (see the file named *Ch 10 World Tech Pro Making it More Real.xlsx*), and saw that their break-even point was in year 2. They also noted that the break-even calculations to the right of the income statement included only their retail sales and not the service sales, although a quick scan of the financial statement totals showed a net loss in year 1 and profits in each year after that. That meant that, even if the break-even calculations in the chart included their service sales, the break-even point would still be during year 2.

The Garcias were much happier with a break-even point in year 2 instead of year 5, where it was prior to improving the realism of their financial model.

The couple realized that Tech World Pro was not yet a business as it had yet to start. It was still only an idea on paper. However, they wanted to estimate a value for the business so they could set up their capitalization table to keep track of who would own what proportion of shares in the business and what the estimated value of the shares would be in March of their first year (three months after they began to set up their business and after their first month of projected sales) after all the projected equity investment was presumed to have been invested in the company.

As shown on the **Valuation Worksheet**, the Garcias compiled a chart showing the net income before interest and taxes had been deducted, a running average of that net income, a multiple, the net income figures multiplied by the multiple, the year-end loan balance amounts, the equity investments into the business in each year, the equity buyback amounts, and the projected dividends.

After considering the three primary ways to estimate a value for a business (see Chapter 8), the Garcias decided that they would apply a version of the income approach by calculating a net present value using a 10% discount rate and their $50,000 investment in the company plus the first three years of net income as the cash flow amounts. As shown on the **Valuation Worksheet**, this calculation generated an initial valuation of $195,179. After adding the $366,000 in projected additional investments from family, the total valuation became $561,179.

Using the **CapTable Worksheet**, Talia and Malik prepared a capitalization table. It showed that the initial valuation (before investments from family) divided by an assumed number of 1,000 shares meant that Talia and Malik would own 1,000 shares valued at $195.18 each. By dividing the new investment by family members of $366,000 by the $195.18 value per share, the couple discovered that would represent 1,879 shares. That meant that Talia and Malik would own 35% of the shares and the family members would own the remaining 65%. When this was further broken down by how much money the family members invested in the business, it showed that Talia's parents would own 47% of the shares and her aunt would own 18%. The couple felt that they had calculated a reasonable valuation for their business, and had adequately figured out which investors would own what proportion of the business.

The Garcias then used the **IRRcalc Worksheet** to calculate the internal rate of return generated by the business, using Excel's "=XIRR" function. That calculation indicated that the overall rate of return would be 23.7% on the $416,000 investment (including the $50,000 contributed by Talia and Malik) into the business during its first three months and the $785,000 of dividends shown on the projected financial statements at the starts of years 2, 3, 4, and 5, and at the end of year 5.

Cross-Chapter Case Activities—Part 11

1. Using this file, **Ch 10 World Tech Pro Making it More Real.xlsx**, consider the calculations and logic used by the Garcias to calculate the business valuation, share allocation and valuation, and internal rate of return.

- Discuss how appealing the business would look as an investment for Talia's parents and aunt.
- Discuss how appealing the business would look as an investment by Talia and Malik.

2. Considering the investment analysis and the ratios, discuss how desirable the business likely looks to Talia and Malik as something to which they might devote a significant part of their life work.

Chapter 12

Finishing the Business Plan

Overview

The last stage of business plan development is to finalize the parts of the plan that must be finished last and to polish its look for targeted readers (Figure 19).

First Things Last

Finalize Major Goals

As contradictory as it might sound, it is after the business plan is almost finished that the entrepreneur can complete the Major Goals section. They should select a limited set of outcomes shown in the plan, perhaps five to 10, to frame as goals that will appeal to targeted investors and other readers.

The major goals should be substantive and relevant. They should be written using a format designed to maximize their impact on targeted readers. The RUMBA (realistic, understandable, measurable, believable, and achievable) formula provides a useful guideline for developing goals. The following are examples of goals that follow the RUMBA formula:

ZYX Company will breakeven by October 2023 after which the company will generate profit increases of 18%, 12%, and 14% for the three years ending in December 2026.

ABC Company will secure a $181,050 loan in May 2022 to finance the new DEF machine needed to produce product GHI to for its introduction to the market in August of that year.

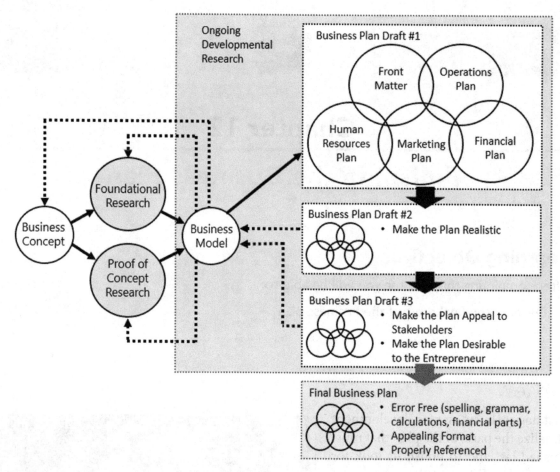

Figure 19. Finishing the Business Plan

(Illustration by Lee A. Swanson)

Include goals in the Major Goals section of the business plan that provide essential information to targeted investors to help them make their decisions about whether or not to invest in the business. Avoid including statements that sound like goals, but are instead a means to achieve a goal. For example, it is probably not relevant to targeted investors if the entrepreneur includes a goal to hire a new employee at a particular time. However, hiring the employee might help the company launch a new product that will help it increase its profits in that and later years. It might be useful to potential investors to frame that outcome as a goal.

Write the Executive Summary

The last part of the business plan the entrepreneurs should write is the *Executive Summary*. Unlike most other types of documents, the executive summary at the start of a business plan can be up to about three pages in length.

As the executive summary might be the first section that targeted readers go through, it must be written to appeal to them. It should provide those readers with information that will encourage them to seriously consider taking the desired action, like investing in the venture. If the contents of the executive summary do not interest readers, they might not go through the rest of the plan and consider investing in the venture.

Last Things Last

Throughout the analyses sections of the plan, the entrepreneur should take control of the narrative when they provide their written interpretations of the analyses results. They can only do this after the plan is almost complete. Entrepreneurs must provide written explanations describing the relevant messages the potential investors and other business plan readers should take from the ratio, breakeven, and critical success factors and sensitivity analyses. Finally, they should polish the plan by proofreading it to eliminate errors and, if relevant, include a capitalization table.

Explain the Ratio Analysis

Entrepreneurs must always include a written analysis and interpretation of what the ratios mean. It is never sufficient only to present the ratios. The entrepreneur should explain to the targeted readers what they believe the ratios indicate and how they show the venture is an excellent investment opportunity. If the potential investment looks promising, investors will analyze the plan on their own; however, investors might not consider the opportunity worth examining if the entrepreneur has not shown their analysis.

When possible, business plan writers should compare the plan's ratios with available industry average ratios and with norms they might find from available sources. If the business has been running for a few years, the entrepreneur should compare ratios from projected statements with actual ratios from past years.

Explain the Break-Even Analysis

A break-even analysis is not an analysis if the entrepreneur only presents it as a set of calculations (see Chapter 8). They must include written explanations for the readers.

An alternative approach to calculating breakeven using formulas is to make a copy of the month–by–month cash flow statements and then delete the lines showing investments, asset purchases, and other nonincome statement items. By converting a cash flow statement into a month-by-month income statement and noting the time when revenues begin to exceed expenses, the entrepreneur can often uncover new information about the business's projected break-even point that is unavailable through formula calculations alone.

Explain the Critical Success Factors and Sensitivity Analysis

Chapter 8 describes the process for conducting a sensitivity analysis. Once finished, the entrepreneur should provide a written explanation indicating its implications.

Finalize and Explain the Business Valuation

Before an entrepreneur can offer a proportion of ownership in a business in exchange for a particular investment amount, they have to have determined a value for the business. Review Chapter 8 for information on the ways in which to calculate the value of a business.

The entrepreneur should provide a written explanation indicating how they arrived at the estimated business valuation.

Finalize the Capitalization Table

See Chapter 8 for information on the capitalization table, a summary of the proportions of ownership each investor in the business has after each new investment in the business.

Polish It Up!

Thoroughly proofread the completed business plan and fix all errors before submitting it to anyone. It is usually best to have other people proofread the work as they will catch errors the writer may miss. Never underestimate the negative consequences that can occur from distributing shoddy work.

The final business plan should have an appealing layout, be bound or otherwise packaged so it stays together and is easy for readers to go through, and include a cover with appropriate visuals.

Write a Letter of Transmittal

A letter of transmittal is to a business plan what a cover letter is to a resume. A letter of transmittal should briefly introduce the business plan to the intended recipient and persuasively, but briefly, communicate the reasons why they should read it.

The letter of transmittal should be tailored to each reader to whom the entrepreneur distributed the business plan. It should be succinct and include what the entrepreneur seeks from the reader, usually funding. It should not summarize the business plan, as that is the job of the executive summary.

References

Review the "Establishing and Maintaining Credibility" section in Chapter 1 for information on using a formal referencing method, like APA, in the business plan. The entrepreneur must include in-text citations throughout the plan wherever they included information they got from some source. Each in-text citation must have a matching reference in the reference list located under this heading in the business plan.

Chapter Summary

After all of the hard work involved with developing a business plan, it must be appropriately finished to have the intended impact with its targeted readers. Before distributing it to investors and other recipients, the entrepreneur should include a limited number of goals in the Major Goals section near the start of the plan. Those goals should be carefully crafted to appeal to intended readers. The entrepreneur should finish the analyses sections of the plan and add written explanations including their interpretations of the analyses results. The final writing task is to develop an executive summary that will entice targeted readers to examine the rest of the plan in detail and consider investing in the venture. After that, the plan should be thoroughly proofread and revised to ensure there are no errors in it. After writing customized letters of transmittal to introduce the plan to targeted readers, the entrepreneur can distribute it.

Exercises

Exercise 12.1—Finishing the Business Plan

Write the final sections of the business plan, as described in Chapter 11, and polish it up for distribution to targeted readers.

Exercise 12.2—Preparing the Letter of Transmittal

Write a letter of transmittal template to use when customizing letters for targeted readers.

Chapter 13

The Business Plan Pitch

Learning Objectives

After completing this chapter, you will be able to:

◆ Deliver an effective business plan pitch

Overview

Writing a good business plan will only get an entrepreneur so far. To achieve their goals, they must be prepared to present their plan effectively to targeted investors and other potential stakeholders. The presentations are usually called pitches, or sometimes elevator pitches because an entrepreneur should be prepared to deliver one in the length of time it takes to ride up a few floors in an elevator with a potential investor. The goal of a pitch is not to fully describe a business idea, but to convince a potential investor in five minutes or less that they should meet with the entrepreneur to learn more about the idea, and potentially invest in it.

© Gorodenkoff/Shutterstock.com

The Pitch

The business plan pitch must focus on what the targeted audience and business plan readers need to know. Usually the pitch will be designed to capture a potential investor's interest so that they will want to talk to the entrepreneur in more depth about investing in the venture. In that case, the pitch should follow a process similar to the one described next.

Entrepreneurs should prepare their pitches, seek feedback on their likely effectiveness, and practice them at every opportunity. The pitch should include enough information to interest prospective investors, but not so much that the message gets lost in the presentation.

Pitches should be developed using the following general script:

1. Describe the market problem that the venture solves.

   The venture should solve a problem for an identifiable group of people or organizations that recognize they have a problem—or can easily be convinced they have one—and are willing to spend money on a solution.

2. Describe how the venture solves the problem.

   The solution the entrepreneur offers should be better than the alternative solutions provided by competitors. It should also be a solution that cannot or will not be readily copied by existing or new competitors.

3. The entrepreneur should explain how and why they and their venture are capable of solving the problem while also generating a profit.

   Potential investors are more likely to consider the entrepreneur to be capable of delivering on the promise if the venture has a strong team, relevant experience, and access to scarce or unique resources or networks.

4. The entrepreneur should explain why they need the financing and anything else they ask for from the potential investors, like their expertise or access to their networks.

   The likelihood of getting funding improves when the entrepreneur can show that the money will increase the business's capacity to deliver on the promise.

5. Describe why the investors should invest in the venture.

   Potential investors want to know how and when they will get their investment back and how much of a return they will earn on their money. The entrepreneur should provide them with an estimate of how much the venture is worth and will be worth in the future. They should carefully explain to the potential investors what is in it for them if they invest in the company.

Chapter Summary

The five-step business plan pitch format described in this chapter can help entrepreneurs engage with targeted investors and convince them to consider investing in ventures. The purpose of the business plan pitch is to, within a short period, capture the attention and interest of targeted investors. A successful pitch should result in invitations from potential investors for the entrepreneur to provide more information about the business.

Exercises

Exercise 13.1—Preparing the Pitch

Prepare a business plan pitch from a completed business plan.

References

Barney, J. B. (1997). *Gaining and sustaining competitive advantage*. Reading, MA: Addison-Wesley.

Barney, J. B., & Hesterly, W. S. (2006). *Strategic management and competitive advantage: Concepts and cases*. Upper Saddle River, NJ: Pearson/Prentice Hall.

Brooks, A. C. (2009). *Social entrepreneurship: A modern approach to social value creation*. Upper Saddle River, NJ: Pearson/Prentice Hall.

Chatterjee, S. (2013). Simple rules for designing business models. *California Management Review, 55*(2), 97–124.

Government of Canada. (2019). *Business plan guide*. Retrieved from http://www.cbo-eco.ca/en/index.cfm/planning/writing-a-business-plan/business-plan-guide/

Hindle, K., & Mainprize, B. (2006). A systematic approach to writing and rating entrepreneurial business plans. *The Journal of Private Equity, 9*(3), 7–23.

Kier, A. S., & McMullen, J. S. (2018). Entrepreneurial imaginativeness in new venture ideation. *Academy of Management Journal, 61*(6), 2265–2295. doi:10.5465/amj.2017.0395

Magretta, J. (2002, May). Why business models matter. *Harvard Business Review, 80*, 86–92.

Mitchell, R. K. (2000). *Introduction to the venture analysis standards 2000: New Venture Template™ Workbook*. Victoria, BC, Canada: International Centre for Venture Expertise.

Osterwalder, A., Pigneur, Y., & Clark, T. (2010). *Business model generation: A handbook for visionaries, game changers, and challengers*. Hoboken, NJ: Wiley.

Porter, M. E. (1985). *Competitive advantage: Creating and sustaining superior performance*. New York, NY: Free Press.

Porter, M. E. (1996). What is strategy? *Harvard Business Review, 74*(6), 61–78.

Ries, E. (2011). *The lean startup: How today's entrepreneurs use continuous innovation to create radically successful businesses*. New York, NY: Crown Business.

Stats Link Canada. (2009). *Financial performance indicators for Canadian business*. Retrieved from http://www.gdsourcing.ca/FPI-Small.PDF

Vesper, K. H. (1996). *New venture experience* (revised ed.). Seattle, WA: Vector Books.

Appendix A

Research Analyses Worksheets

Purpose

These worksheets are designed to help business plan writers save time and become more focused on the essential tasks associated with conducting the research required to complete business plans.

Key-Questions-First Approach

Some business plan writers make the mistake of starting the research part of their work by applying an analysis tool—like a PESTEL (political, economic, social, technological, environmental, and legal) analysis, Porter's five forces model, or SWOT/TOWS framework—before they first identify what they need to know. To save themselves much work and to focus their research on the right questions, they should first develop a list of the critical questions for which they require answers.

The Research Analysis Worksheets apply a *key-questions first* approach. They provide a tool for researchers to use to first craft sets of crucial questions for which they need answers for each of the three overlapping categories of business plan research, as shown in Figure 4 in Chapter 2 of this book. After compiling the sets of critical questions, researchers should seek targeted answers for them by applying the tools designed for each of the four levels of analysis described in Chapter 2, while ensuring they use the right tools for the right level of analysis.

As explained in Chapter 2, each of the three categories of business plan research has a distinct purpose. *Proof of concept* and *foundational research* support business model and business plan development. *Ongoing developmental research* focuses more on business plan development, although it also helps entrepreneurs make continual and necessary adjustments to the business model.

The following sections describe the overall questions each of the three types of business plan research approaches address.

Proof of Concept Research

Proof of concept research addresses the following question: *Can the business concept be converted into a viable and sustainable business entity?*

Entrepreneurs and investors require an affirmative answer to this question before they will be willing to develop the concept into a business. Refer to Chapter 2 for information on conducting proof of concept research.

See the worksheets for a sample list of the key questions to which entrepreneurs need answers to determine whether a business concept can be developed into a viable and sustainable business.

Foundational Research

Foundational research seeks to answer the following question: *What resources—including time, knowledge, people, money, equipment, and facilities—and investment are required to convert the business concept into a viable and sustainable business entity?*

The answers to this question support business model development, help verify that a business concept can become a viable and ongoing venture, and provide entrepreneurs with information about the resources needed to start and operate the business. See Chapter 2 for a discussion on the types of information foundational research should uncover for entrepreneurs.

See the worksheets for a sample list of the key questions to which entrepreneurs need answers related to their business's resource and financing needs.

Ongoing Developmental Research

Ongoing developmental research seeks to get increasingly accurate answers to the following question: *What resources and investment are required to efficiently and effectively set up, start up, and sustain ongoing business operations?*

While foundational research focuses on acquiring the needed resourcing and financing answers to ensure that the business can be viable and sustainable, ongoing developmental research asks more detailed questions to support business plan development, including the strategies the business will implement. The results from ongoing developmental research should also continually alert entrepreneurs to the need to make the adjustments to the business model and to uncover what those adjustments should be. Read Chapter 2 for information on conducting ongoing developmental research.

See the worksheets for a sample list of the key questions to which entrepreneurs need answers to develop efficient and effective business strategies for the set up, start up, and ongoing operations phases of business development.

Using the Right Tool for Right Level of Analysis

As shown in Figure 8 in Chapter 2, there are four levels of analysis, each with their own tools. The worksheets provide you with some guidance on how to apply the different levels of analysis.

Secondary Information Sources

Primary research involves talking to experts, conducting market surveys, and taking other action to get needed information for business plan development from real people. It is always a good first step when developing a business plan to seek assistance from experts in the field. Business plan writers can save a significant amount of time and effort by asking these experts for their advice.

Secondary research involves collecting information that is available through libraries, websites, information repositories, and other places. The following table summarizes some of the sources for secondary information along with information on the purposes, validity, usefulness, and benefits from using the listed sources.

Source	Purpose	Validity	Useful	Increases Strength	Referencing
Academic articles	To add credibility to the plan	High	Sometimes	Usually	APA
Competitor websites	Information on competitors' products, locations, prices, etc.	Usually high	Usually essential	Yes	APA
Potential supplier catalogue sites	To get prices will need to pay for required assets (include taxes, duties, shipping costs, etc.)	Usually high	Usually essential	Yes	APA
Valid sources for market research (IBISWorld, etc.)	Secondary market research	High if the source is good	Essential, but the source must be good	Yes	APA
Valid sources for understanding the operating environment (Statistics Canada, IBISWorld, community profiles, etc.)	Provide needed context for the plan	High if the source is good	Essential, but the source must be good	Yes	APA

Source	Purpose	Validity	Useful	Increases Strength	Referencing
Valid sources for projecting sales, cost increases, and other numbers	Provide support for projections and other figures	High if the source is good	Essential, but the source must be good	Yes	APA
Industry or association or specialized sources specific to the industry or as a source to address a particular question	Often used to supply needed information not available through other sources or to provide context or support projections	High if the source is good	Sometimes if the source is excellent and the information is required	Often	APA
General or random websites

News stories posted online or in newspapers or magazines | Often used to provide context or support projections—but the information in these sites is sometimes not valid. However, if the source uses excellent data, it is better to go to the actual source for the information | Often low | Often not, unless the source is verified or established as being of use for the particular purpose for which it is used | Sometimes | APA |

The Worksheets

Use the following worksheets to develop the critical questions to help guide your business plan research. Determine the types of analyses required to adequately address each key question, as shown in the examples provided.

Worksheet 1—Proof of Concept Key Questions

Can the business concept be converted into a viable and sustainable business entity?	
Key Questions (examples)	Levels of Analysis and Tools
What specific value proposition elements—perhaps like reductions in operating costs, reduced risk of injuries, and increased accuracy and reliability of operating processes—do we need to prove to potential investors, and what type of proof is needed (e.g., reasonable cost reduction estimates, estimates of gained employee workdays due to reduced injuries, and estimated revenue increases due to improvements in operating processes)?	Societal-Level Trends • PESTEL Analysis Industry-Level Trends • Porter's Five-Forces Model Market-Level Trends • 5C Marketing Analysis • Market Profile Analysis Organization-Level Trends • Founder Fit • SWOT/TOWS • Financial Projections • Core Competency Analysis Other • VRIO Framework • Interviews with experts • Market surveys
What would it take for a company to replace what they do now with this solution? Would they need to take measures like replacing existing people or equipment, and what other challenges do they face in adopting this solution?	Market-Level Trends • 5C Marketing Analysis • Market Profile Analysis Organization-Level Trends • SWOT/TOWS • Financial Projections • Core Competency Analysis Other • VRIO (valuable, rare, inimitable, and organized) Framework • Interviews with experts
How many potential customers are there? How much is each potential customer likely to buy?	Industry-Level Trends • Porter's Five-Forces Model Market-Level Trends • 5C Marketing Analysis • Market Profile Analysis Other • Interviews with experts • Market surveys
What other solutions are there that deliver similar results? How much do they cost relative to this idea? What are the advantages and disadvantages of each possible solution, of which this idea is one?	Market-Level Trends • 5C Marketing Analysis • Market Profile Analysis Other • Interviews with experts • Market surveys

Worksheet 2—Foundational Research Key Questions

What resources—including time, knowledge, people, money, equipment, and facilities— and investment are required to convert the business concept into a viable and sustainable business entity?	
Key Questions (examples)	Levels of Analysis and Tools
What fixed assets, including equipment and machinery, must be purchased before this business can start? How much does the entrepreneur expect all of this to cost (more precise costs can be determined through ongoing developmental research)? How long will it take to order, install, test, and make sure that the equipment and machinery will work as needed (before start-up)?	Other • Supplier websites and catalogues • Interviews with experts
What are the average salaries and wages for the categories of employees in the industry for the geographic region?	Industry- and Market-Level Trends • Published Average Salaries Other • Interviews with experts
What is the optimum mix of pricing, distribution, promotions, and product decisions to best appeal to how the targeted customers make their buying decisions?	Societal-Level Trends • PESTEL Analysis Industry-Level Trends • Porter's Five-Forces Model Market-Level Trends • 5C Marketing Analysis • Market Profile Analysis Other • Interviews with experts • Market surveys
Does the entrepreneur need to be concerned mainly with direct competitors, or does their kind of business also need to worry about customers choosing to spend their money on indirect competitors' products and services instead of on the entrepreneur's products or services?	Societal-Level Trends • PESTEL Analysis Industry-Level Trends • Porter's Five-Forces Model Market-Level Trends • 5C Marketing Analysis • Market Profile Analysis Other • Interviews with experts • Market surveys
In what ways will the entrepreneur communicate with their targeted customers? When will they communicate with them? What specific messages do they plan to convey to targeted customers? How much will this promotions plan cost?	Societal-Level Trends • PESTEL Analysis Industry-Level Trends • Porter's Five-Forces Model

What resources—including time, knowledge, people, money, equipment, and facilities—and investment are required to convert the business concept into a viable and sustainable business entity?	
Key Questions (examples)	Levels of Analysis and Tools
	Market-Level Trends • 5C Marketing Analysis • Market Profile Analysis Other • Interviews with experts • Market surveys
To what risks is the business exposed? How will the entrepreneur mitigate each of the risks they have identified? When transferring risks through insurance, what kinds of insurance do they need to purchase and how much will this cost (more precise costs can be determined through ongoing developmental research)?	Societal-Level Trends • PESTEL Analysis Industry-Level Trends • Porter's Five-Forces Model Market-Level Trends • 5C Marketing Analysis • Market Profile Analysis Other • Interviews with experts
What decisions does the entrepreneur need to make and include in a partnership agreement or articles of incorporation to make sure that the business partners account for all of the likely scenarios related to ownership transfers and buyouts?	Societal-Level Trends • PESTEL Analysis Industry-Level Trends • Porter's Five-Forces Model Market-Level Trends • 5C Marketing Analysis • Market Profile Analysis Organization-Level Trends • Founder Fit • SWOT/TOWS • Financial Projections • Core Competency Analysis Other • Interviews with experts

Worksheet 3—Ongoing Developmental Research Key Questions

What resources and investment are required to efficiently and effectively set up, start up, and sustain ongoing business operations?	
Key Questions (examples)	Levels of Analysis and Tools
What are the precise costs for the fixed assets the entrepreneur needs to purchase (backed up by references to industrial equipment and similar catalogues)?	Other • Supplier websites and catalogues • Interviews with experts
What are the precise costs for the needed insurance (backed up by a quotation from an insurance broker)?	Other • Quotes from insurance companies • Published industry averages • Interviews with experts
What are the correct wage and salary costs for the human resources the entrepreneur needs to hire (backed up by data indicating the wage and salary amounts for comparable positions in the region in which the company will operate)?	Industry- and Market-Level Trends • Published Average Salaries Other • Interviews with experts
What are the assumptions and methods used to project revenues (backed up by evidence that the assumptions and methods are realistic)?	Other • Published industry averages • Interviews with experts • Market surveys
What are the precise costs for the inventories the entrepreneur needs to purchase before they can start the business (backed up by evidence from wholesale catalogues and quotations from targeted suppliers)?	Other • Quotes from suppliers • Wholesale catalogues • Published industry averages • Interviews with experts

Worksheet 4—Research Planning

1. Develop a research plan that clusters the questions for which you need answers according to the sources for that information (see Worksheet 1).

2. Establish a timeline for conducting the research by including dates by which you want the results from your inquiries and research work.

    Note that while you can access websites and public information at almost anytime, you must plan some lead time for meeting with experts and getting quotes from professionals (like insurance agents) and other suppliers. You must also allow lead time if planning to conduct market surveys.

3. Consider where you can go to get other people to conduct some of your research. Some government agencies have business resource centers that conduct some types of research for entrepreneurs. Often those agencies have access to useful research databases.

4. Implement your research plan.

Appendix B

Business Plan Word Template

Please go to the inside front cover for information on how to access the Business Plan Word Template.

© Muk Photo/Shutterstock.com

Appendix C

Business Plan Excel Template

Please go to the inside front cover for information on how to access the Business Plan Excel Template.

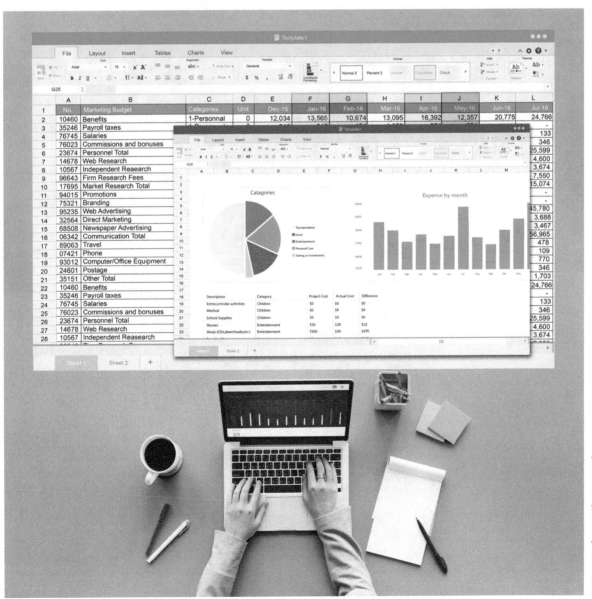

Appendix D

Common Expenses

© Michal Chmurski/Shutterstock.com

- Advertising and promotions
- Credit and debit card machines costs
- Donations
- Hospitality (for visitors and guests)
  - Meals, hotel rooms, liquor
- Insurance
  - Key person
  - Liability
  - Property
  - Vehicle
- Internet and Wi-Fi costs
- Maintenance and repairs
  - Building
  - Office machinery and equipment (photocopier, computers, furniture)
  - Production equipment

- o Vehicle
- o Website
- Meetings and events
  - o Equipment rentals
  - o Room rentals
  - o Tradeshow expenses
  - o Travel
- Ownership expenses
  - o Property taxes
  - o Routine maintenance on properties
- Point of sale terminal costs
- Renewals
  - o Business license
  - o Domain name
  - o Memberships (Chamber of Commerce and professional and industry associations)
  - o Professional fees
  - o Subscriptions
- Rentals
  - o Facility lease
  - o Parking spaces
  - o Storage
- Services
  - o Accounting
  - o Banking fees
  - o Garbage disposal
  - o Information technology systems
  - o Janitorial
  - o Legal
  - o Machinery
  - o Music streaming
  - o Recycling fees
  - o Security monitoring
  - o Social media and website maintenance
  - o Snow removal
- Supplies
  - o Cleaning (detergent, mops, brooms, vacuum bags, cloths)
  - o Decorations
  - o First aid supplies

- o Office (pens, paper, photocopier toner, staplers and staples, hole punchers, binders, file folders)
- o Small tools
- o Staff room(cutlery, plates, coffee, and filters)
- o Uniforms
- o Washroom (towels, soap, toilet paper)
- Training and professional development
  - o Health and safety
  - o Productivity
- Travel
  - o Flights
  - o Gasoline
  - o Insurance
  - o Meals
  - o Parking
  - o Per diem
  - o Vehicle rentals
- Utilities
  - o Electrical
  - o Internet
  - o Natural gas
  - o Telephone—cell
  - o Telephone—landline phone
  - o Water and sewer